THE GOLDY SHUFFLE

the Bill Goldsworthy story

THE GOLDY SHUFFLE

the Bill Goldsworthy story

by
Richard Rainbolt and Ralph Turtinen

T.S. DENISON & COMPANY, INC.
Minneapolis

 T. S. DENISON & COMPANY, INC.

Standard Book Number 513-01226-5

Library of Congress Card Number: 70-180924

Printed in the United States of America

by The Brings Press

Published by T. S. Denison & Company, Inc.

Copyright © MCMLXXI by Richard Rainbolt and Ralph Turtinen

Minneapolis, Minn. 55437

Contents

ACKNOWLEDGEMENT

The authors and the publishers wish to gratefully acknowledge the cooperation and assistance of the management of the North Stars without whose constant assistance and cooperation this book would not have been possible. Unless otherwise credited all photographs herein are official North Star photographs.

FOREWORD

This book might have been titled "Tempest on Right Wing."

Bill Goldsworthy has been a powerful, ofttimes turbulent force on right wing for the Minnesota North Stars.

Moreover, from a time in his early youth, when he roamed the streets of Kitchener, Ontario, as a leader of a gang of toughs known as the Falcons until his third full season in the National Hockey League, Goldy was caught up by an inner tempest that hurled him recklessly through life.

That he possessed considerable hockey talent, a singular desire to succeed in the sport, and a gentle manner off the ice — particularly with younger people — too often was obscured by the fury of the tempest.

As a result, some people gave up on him. Some did not.

While those who did not falter in their faith can be credited with some of the successes Goldy has enjoyed, it was he alone who ultimately harnessed that inner something that had prevented his achieving the potential hockey people knew he had.

This book relates the internal and external conflicts

of a young man to whom success has come neither easily nor painlessly.

Realistically, it is important not to maximize nor minimize his athletic achievements to date. Goldy, today, is at a point in his career that could catapult him to the super-stardom many predict. Time will determine that.

Goldy and Cesare Maniago are the only two remaining charter members of Minnesota's original expansion team which, in its four years of existence, has seen seventy-eight others wear the green, gold and white.

The longevity of the two is an expression of the faith and confidence General Manager Wren Blair always felt toward them — through bad times and good.

Wren has played a key role in Goldy's growth. Their periodic conflicts — some bombastic, some comical — are almost legend. Yet their mutual survival in these colorful confrontations is indicative of the respect each has for the other's abilities and goals.

The Goldy Shuffle, a carefree act of happy showmanship, is but a symbol of Goldy's tumultuous career. Its existence is its only significance. As so many other dramatic happenings in his life, the shuffle was a creation of impulse.

It might never have been born, because the path he traveled in his formative years was strewn with danger and pitfalls.

There was a serious knee injury that required two operations; a slash across the face that nearly cost him an eye; a full-flight crash into a goal post that split his arm open to the bone and three collisions on ice that rendered Goldy unconscious. The last mishap led to the use of a helmet.

But these were physical hazards, something every hockey player must anticipate because of the punishing nature of the game.

Goldy had that other thing to combat as well, that inner conflict that had separated who he was from who he could be. Overcoming this, as many people in many professions must do to climb to the top, is perhaps the greatest success story of Goldy's career, whatever his future accomplishments.

The development of this book has been a cooperative effort of the authors and Bill Goldsworthy.

The writers thank the North Stars, particularly president Walter L. Bush, Jr., General Manager Wren Blair, and Public Relations Director Dick Dillman, for their considerate and courteous assistance in preparing the manuscript. Wren's personal appraisal of the North Stars' progress and future possibilities is contained in "A Word from The Bird," as an epilogue.

In addition we are personally appreciative of our respective families for their encouragement and enthusiasm.

Above all we are indebted to Bill and June Goldsworthy for their graciousness, patience and creative contributions to The Goldy Shuffle.

Richard Rainbolt
Ralph Turtinen

Chapter I

Thoroughbred on Skates

There were two things in life that Wren Blair had always been inflexible about: he could not tolerate losing, and he would not accept mediocre performances from young men who he knew were capable of much greater things. Known among hockey people as "The Bird," Blair had always been more hawk than dove in his approach to the game. If he erupted in anger on occasions, as he had been known to do, it was due to a peculiar passion he had for winning. He spent the better part of his life scheming how to win hockey games, and if there were a flaw in his strategy, he would invoke the wrath of the gods of hockey to drive his men to victory by sheer determination or anger.

But he was also an astute hockey man, much respected throughout his native Canada, and because of his accomplishments in 1958 he was named Hockey Executive of the Year.

While Blair did, of necessity, accept losing (but only in retrospect), he could not be so flexible in the matter of young men who were not producing to their full capability. He spent many years experimenting with techniques that would reach into the soul of a young man and drive him to achieve heights he, the young man, did not know he was capable of reaching. This did not always endear Blair to the particular young man he was driving, at first, and only years later, upon looking back to what had happened, did many of his players come to recognize that at least part of their success had been due to The Bird being unable to accept less than their best.

There was a kid from Kitchener, Ontario — a tall, blonde kid with powerful, sloping shoulders and a temper every bit as explosive as that of Mr. Blair, who particularly irked The Bird, because he knew that somewhere deep inside this firebrand were the ingredients of a mighty fine hockey player. The Bird devised various techniques to probe for these ingredients.

There would be 15,000 loyal fans watching and the Minnesota North Stars were not performing in a manner entirely satisfactory to them or The Bird. Blair was particularly annoyed by the big kid on right wing, but instead of sending out an entire new line as most coaches in professional hockey do when they want to vent their wrath on a specific player, he sent out one man on right wing. There was no mistaking who the rebuke was intended for as the solitary figure skated to the bench.

"You sit here, Goldy," said The Bird, talking politely over the shoulder of the angry winger, "you're too tired to be out there and the other guys have to wait for you to catch up to them. I don't want to overwork you tonight."

Goldy's line came off and went back on the ice for two more shifts without him, and by this time he was seething, kicking the boards in anger and talking straight ahead toward the ice, the words really intended for the curly-haired coach behind him. Blair ignored the words, unless there was something he could pick up and needle him with.

When The Bird figured Goldy was really mad, he would lean over his shoulder once more.

"Goldy, would it be too much if I asked you to play one more shift tonight? I know you're tired ..."

Goldy stormed over the boards, knocked down nine players and an official, walked in on the goalie, pulled him out of the nets, and scored the game-winning goal. With a big smile of satisfaction on his face, he skated back to the bench.

"You idiot," said Blair, turning his back on the big forward.

The technique had variations to it, but it was always spiced with the same kind of sarcasm.

"I've put the needle to Goldy so bad that sometimes it comes out on the other side," said The Bird. "I took the position that there was no way I was going to let that kid screw up, even if I had to take him apart at the seams, which I did a few times. He's like a thoroughbred horse. Some of them you can pat on the head and some of them you have to put the whip to. You have to use the whip on Goldy.

"Sure we've had our run-ins. If you really care for someone and you want him to be successful, you're going to be tougher on him than someone else. I believe that discipline is a very big part of love. It's hard to do. When you discipline someone very close to you, it hurts you as much as him. But if you love him enough, and he deserves it, then you better well do it, and fast.

"Goldy's temper is one of the things that has gotten him into trouble, but it's also one of the things I like about him. He has spirit, and that helps in hockey. His problem was that he didn't know how to harness his temper. He's learning though, and this could make him a great hockey player."

In their first year with the North Stars, Blair began working his psychology on Goldy.

"You know what really annoys me about you," said The Bird in a practice session, "is that you could be as good as Bobby Hull if you wanted to bad enough."

"Are you kidding?" asked Goldy, smiling.

"No, I'm not kidding, I'm damned serious!"

Their relationship would be stormy in the years to come because Blair had never been known to be timid about applying the whip if that's what was necessary to get the most out of his horses, thorough-bred or not.

"One night," said The Bird, "I got mad at him and pulled him off the ice just before the end of the period. He was the last man on the bench, and I was going to open the door onto the ice, not knowing the buzzer was about to go off. When it did, Goldy stood up quickly to go up the ramp and ran right into me. I bounced off and then I started back at him.

"Danny O'Shea grabbed me, and Stan Waylett, our trainer, was holding on to Goldy, and I was shouting around Danny and saying 'Did you run into me on purpose?' Danny said to me, 'Come on, he didn't run into you.' So I started up the stairs and turned around and said, 'If you ever take a step at me ...' You know, he was standing way up over me on skates, and it must have been comical.

"I went into my office and nothing further was said, but when the game was over I went to the dressing room and Goldy was bending over taking off his skates. I said to him, kiddingly, 'Did I hurt you when I ran into you up there?' He just looked at me and said, 'Oh, Lord,' and rolled his eyes. Sometimes you do and say things for fun to break the tension, so I said, 'I'm sorry, Goldy, if I ever hit you hard ...' Then he started to laugh and everyone in the room broke up."

On the way out of the dressing room that night, Goldy crossed paths with Blair once more.

"I don't think I tried to run into you," said Goldy.

"Oh, that doesn't matter, forget it," said Blair.

Goldy frowned for a moment, then said: "Why is it always me? I'm always in trouble."

Chapter II

Flight of the Falcon

Kitchener, Ontario is not known as a breeding ground of thoroughbreds. It's a community of 125,000 persons located in southern Ontario, just northeast of Detroit. Its primary industry is dairy products.

One of the city's best known athletes in the 1930s and early 40s was a pretty fair baseball pitcher by the name of Art Goldsworthy. Art had also impressed the locals with his hockey ability, but in uncharacteristic manner for a Canadian, he had given up the sport after two seasons, and devoted his time to baseball.. Some said Art Goldsworthy could have been a heck of a fine hockey player. Maybe even qualify for a major league. Every town in every province of Canada has had its boy who could have been in major league hockey, if only ...

The odds are lousy. They were lousy on August 24, 1944 when Art and Manetta Goldsworthy gave birth to William Alfred Goldsworthy, who came into the world with a tuft of thin blonde hair that never would get very thick before it started thinning again.

William did not look like a hockey thoroughbred in his early years. He was a skinny kid with over-large ears and a pretty face that would have been great smiling out shyly over a choir robe, but was not the kind you find poking out of a hockey uniform. That was for tough guys.

The Goldsworthy family lived in a large brick house where they boarded hockey players to supplement Art's modest income as a salesman. Bill and his brother, Ken, five years his senior, shared a small bedroom with one bed, which became a source of many scuffles between the two. It was cold in that brick house during those winter nights, and the brothers battled endlessly over possession of the blankets. Their father usually thrust himself into these encounters by directing a flat and swift hand at the posterior of the two antagonists, an action he would come to regret later.

After absorbing many of these lickings, the boys decided they had better work out some sort of truce about the covers. So quite by chance they learned that their father's ties, of which he had four, when tied securely around each corner of the covers and then to the bed posts, prevented one or the other from hogging the warm blankets. All they had to do was crawl under the covers from the top, and they were snug and warm in a kind of envelope-like arrangement.

By morning, when Art Goldsworthy began dressing to go out selling, the ties were knotted and wrinkled, which did nothing for his sartorial splendor as he made his rounds.

Art Goldsworthy was of English lineage, and his wife of German descent, and on Sundays they would take their young sons to a Lutheran Church in Kitchener, then to grandfather's house for dinner. William's grandfather, his mother's father, always put out a glass of cider and a German sausage sandwich for the boys, the latter shored up with a half-inch of horseradish.

"You eat this and you'll never catch a cold," said the grandfather.

Not only did they not catch a cold, but they had a hard time catching their breath as the horseradish burned its way down. Every Sunday when the rest of the devout parishioners in the Lutheran Church were praying for salvation, little William was praying that his grandfather had run out of horseradish.

Whether it was the prospect of confronting that horseradish every Sunday, or not, the family stopped going to church.

At the age of six, when his family was boarding hockey players from the Junior B team known as the Kitchener Canucks, skinny little Bill Goldsworthy laced up his first pair of skates. They were an old pair his father had bought him, but the vintage of the blades meant nothing. He liked them. Bill and his brother skated together a lot, but Ken never was interested in the sport.

There is a dream every boy has, about someday being a great athlete with throngs of admirers cheering him on, and to the Canadian boy the dream is made of skates and sticks and pucks and a slap shot into the nets behind a beaten goalie.

At age seven, Goldy was playing league hockey against the best seven-year-old hockey players in all of Kitchener. The league, like many throughout Canada, was operated by the police department, which one day would spend as much time chasing Goldy down the streets as it did trying to teach him to play his position.

When spring would finally come in the north country and the ice was gone, Goldy played on — in the streets, in the big brick house he was born in, any place where there was a flat surface he could bang a puck or a tennis ball around on. He knew the names of all the greats in the National Hockey League, and of these his idol was the big right winger for the Detroit Red Wings — Gordy Howe. So young Goldy played on the right side. He never had a desire to play anywhere else.

On Saturday night Art Goldsworthy would send Bill out to get some pop, always with the same instructions: "Now you make sure you get cold pop." The family did not have a refrigerator, and they would have to put the soft drinks on a block of ice.

Bill would run the four blocks to the Five Points store and tell the clerk, "The usual six," which meant two orange, a root beer, Pepsi, Coke and a grape. The clerk would take the bottles from a cooler and put them into a carton without wiping off the moisture. This caused the bottom of the carton to become soggy, and sometimes it broke open. When one's bottle broke he was just out of luck. Since William was particularly fond of the orange, he would carry these bottles in his hip pockets as he ran the four blocks home.

Manetta Goldsworthy would cook up a batch of popcorn on those occasions, and Goldy, his brother Ken, and their father would settle in front of the television set for the evening to watch Hockey Night in Canada. It was a ritual that never varied from week to week, except for the particular type of pop Bill might break on the way home.

When the Kitchener-Waterloo Dutchmen, a Canadian senior amateur team, was playing a game in Kitchener, Goldy ran home from school, tossed down his supper, then raced to the arena in time for the arrival of the visiting team's bus. Many other kids had the same idea. They'd wrestle for a player's bag, run in the door of the arena, drop the bag and go hide in a men's room until game time. A couple of bucks was a lot of money for a kid to pay for a hockey game in those days.

Among the players Goldy would remember from those days were a flashy forward named Dave Balon, who one day would become the first draft choice of the Minnesota North Stars in the expansion, and a rangy Italian goaltender with the unlikely hockey name of Cesare Maniago.

Once Goldy saw the famed Whitby Dunlops play a game, and he was fascinated by the turbulent outbursts of their coach, a fiery gentleman by the name of Wren Blair, who paced behind the bench like a caged lion and emitted sounds about as loud. That their careers were on a collision course could not be foreseen at that time because, for one thing,

Goldy was not even a red hot prospect in the kid leagues. Certainly a good young hockey player, but he was not the best on his team. And if you weren't the best in Kitchener, Ontario, dreams of someday reaching the big time were, indeed, preposterous.

Not that these were his only dreams. If you wanted to be big quickly, as a teenager in the community of Kitchener, you made your mark as a leader of one of the gangs that roamed the back streets. Goldy began to run with a group of toughs known as the Falcons. Their status symbol was a jacket with a falcon stitched on the back, and they were one of the meanest outfits around in those days.

Goldy was one of the leaders of the fabled Falcons, because in spite of his lean frame, he was tall for his age and he had always had an explosive temper that struck fear into his peers. The Falcons would prowl lumber yards in the moonlight, gathering materials for their clubhouse, and this bit of petty thievery would be the beginning of greater hits for some of them.

Young William led two lives. At high noon of a given day he might be found in a gravel pit leading the Falcons into a brawl with one of the other kid gangs in those parts. Sometimes these minor skirmishes escalated into bee-bee gun wars.

When they weren't fighting, the Falcons were raiding gardens or committing other small offenses against the citizenry.

One of their favorite targets was the bakery man, who made his rounds with a wagon pulled by a tired old horse. The Falcons would hide behind a house until the horse and wagon ambled up, and when the bakery man went in to make a delivery, they'd spring out to the wagon, snatch some cakes, and be gone before the return of the man. This sport proved to be tiring and not especially challenging at times, so they made slingshots and found that a stone, carefully directed at that end of the horse farthest from its head, caused unusual consequences. The sting of the stone sent the horse galloping off in a great lurch that left cakes strewn about the streets. While the delivery man was racing off in loud pursuit of the beast and the wagon, the Falcons would be collecting cakes off the street.

One day Goldy went into a store and deftly slipped a dozen phonograph records under his Falcon jacket. As skinny as he was, this gave him the appearance of having swallowed, whole, one dozen large pizzas, and it did not go undetected. As he walked out the front door carrying his booty, there was a sickening tap on his shoulder. He was too weighted down with phonograph records to run.

"Son, you come with me," said the floor walker.

Goldy ended up in juvenile court, and if the law was lenient with him that time, the incident did serve to cut into his activities: he was so scared that he never stole anything thereafter.

When he wasn't running with the Falcons, Goldy usually had a hockey stick or a baseball bat or a football in his hands. Very rarely would he be caught holding a school book. He did become interested in history and French, but the more time spent with books meant the less time available for the gravel pits and the arena and other things he was interested in.

The school people gave him guidance tests because they suspected he was capable of doing much better than his grades showed, and that these confirmed their suspicions did not make much of an impact of Goldy. The educators would not make special allowances for athletes, and Goldy just had too many other things going to fret over books and papers.

Hockey was always his primary interest, but he did dabble in other athletics. In 11th grade, though he weighed less than 140 pounds, he went out for the school football team, hoping to become a star running back. They had a scrimmage game, and in the huddle the quarterback looked over at the gangly Goldy and said:

"You're going to get the ball."

Goldy looked up at the huge defensive line pawing the ground like a whole herd of bulls.

"I'll give it a try," he said.

They gave him the ball and the rough ringleader of the Falcons went dashing into the line as though he were leading the charge in the gravel pit. A big defenseman picked him up in a bear hug and carried him ten yards behind the line of scrimmage before depositing him on the turf in an unfriendly manner.

"Have you got another position I can play?" Goldy asked, when they huddled again.

He became a defensive safety, and this was more to his liking because then he would be doing the hitting rather than the other way around, and the contact involved served as a good mental and physical conditioner for hockey.

In those days Goldy would practice football right after school, walk home and eat supper, then head for the hockey rink. There was never much time for homework, and when there was he had little inclination to do it. Anyway, homework was not good for the image if you were a leader of the Falcons.

He had, like his father, given baseball a try, but his mighty swings served only to create some ripples in the summer breezes. Very rarely did he put a ripple in the ball, so he quit. He tried softball, because there the missile was larger and not moving quite so fast, but the results were no better.

The older of the Goldsworthy brothers, Ken, had not been especially attracted to athletics, and at the age of sixteen he quit school to go to work in a tire plant. The family had come to hard times then, and had moved out of the big brick house and into an apartment. Only two years after quitting school, Ken went into the Royal Canadian Air Force, where he became a meterologist and a career military man.

While young Bill was attracting some attention as a bad character among the teen-age set, he was developing a similar image on the ice. Despite his slight dimensions, and the fact that Canadian kids are raised to play a strong body-checking style of hockey, not many players took runs at the blonde skater. Retaliation would be instant and severe, and as he grew larger, his fuse seemed to grow shorter.

Though he was not considered the best hockey player on those kid teams, he was good enough to make the Kitchener All-Star team, which traveled to other cities to play other all-star teams. This made a great impression on him, going into new places where large crowds came out to cheer the local favorites. It also meant less time with that roaming gang of toughs known as the Falcons.

Young Goldy began leaning in a different direction, because instead of running with the gang, he would pack up his duffle bag and walk a mile to catch a bus for practice with the all-star club. If the roads were exceptionally icy, he would take the skates from the bag, put them on, and skate the mile to the bus.

The duffle bag was always well stocked with catalogs and magazines, which he used for shin pads. Before game time he would take them out and tape them to his legs, thus preventing a lot of bruises and charlie horses.

At the age of fourteen Goldy advanced to the midget ranks. He was very near one of those forks in the road of life that every youngster must approach and decide in which direction lies the most adventure.

Every little hamlet, even in the Canadian back country, has a scout nearby, representing one of the major league organizations. It has always been that way in Canada. The scouting system is a key link in a complex chain that has produced the greatest hockey players in the world. Not even the Americans, with their wealth' and organizational genius and their penchant for glorifying their athletes, have been able to crack the system. Not yet.

The scouts saw something in that skinny kid — perhaps his free-wheeling, pell mell style that showed his unbridled spirit — that kept them coming back. He was not a prolific scorer in those days, but when he was on the ice there was always a feeling that what was taking place was a kind of controlled mayhem, and that something was going to happen momentarily.

The scouts' attention filled young Goldy's head with dreams. So he made a decision that thousands of other Canadian boys had made before and after, that he would someday play in the National Hockey League.

Goldy resigned from the Falcons. He had chosen a path that some others in the gang had not had opened to them, or else had declined to travel.

Goldy's parents fed his new dream, but it was a fantasy. The youngster could not even skate particularly well, striding in a stiff-legged manner, and whatever other ingredients go into an NHL player, skating was top priority. Everything else — stick handling, shooting, taking the puck off the boards, checking — would improve with time, but first you had to know how to skate.

Still, he was fast and he had a good shot, and above all, he had desire. The scouts kept coming back to look at the temperamental blonde youngster. So did Goldy's Uncle Lloyd, who was an avid hockey fan and whose one big wish was to live long enough to see his nephew play for the Class B Waterloo Siskins. To Uncle Lloyd, that would be like having kin in the NHL.

Lloyd got his wish. After his second year in the midgets, when he was just sixteen, Goldy was given a tryout with the Siskins. He made the team. Lloyd was so pleased that he promised his nephew one dollar for every goal he scored and 50c for every assist.

This Lloyd came to regret, because in one game young Goldy played like a thoroughbred running away from the field, scoring five goals and seven assists. That cost Uncle Lloyd $8.50, and his wife would not speak to him or her nephew for weeks after that, since she had her heart set on buying a new hat with the money that ended up in Goldy's pocket.

The Siskins won the championship that year, and Goldy's performance, when he was not in the penalty box, gave every indication that he was on the way up. Still, if he were ever to go on to the big time, the young right winger had to overcome two major problems, one mental and one physical: he had to spend less time in the penalty box and more on the ice, by putting the reins on his temper, and he had to learn how to skate. One would plague him for a long time. The other was resolved more easily. He learned how to skate.

Chapter III

A Care Package From Home

To the American, Niagara Falls is known as a haven for honeymooners, not a factory for producing hockey players. To the Canadian, the name suggests both matrimony and mayhem.

The mayhem has long been provided by the Niagara Falls Flyers, a Junior A team in the Boston Bruin organization, and a member of the Ontario Hockey Association, one of the oldest hockey leagues in existence.

Goldy was summoned to Niagara Falls after his year with the Waterloo Siskins. And this is where hundreds of boys in their teens are forced to make a decision that changes the course of their lives. Hockey people say the choice isn't an either/or situation, and that there's no reason a kid can't get a good education and play the game at the same time.

Some even argue that Junior A hockey, which is where most of the professionals receive their apprenticeship, goes out of its way to assure that the aspiring major leaguers continue with their schooling. The same hockey people will say that the guy who cuts it with the pros is the guy with the greatest dedication to the game.

So, while education is there to be had, the Junior A player is dedicated to a singular cause: to make it to the pro ranks.

That was Goldy's ambition. He had given fleeting thoughts to going into education some day, perhaps as a physical education teacher. But when the offer was made to him, there was never any question what the decision would be. The educational route would just have to wait. Goldy was going to chase a dream.

Niagara Falls is but 90 miles south of Kitchener, and Goldy packed his personal belongings in late summer of 1962 and left home for the first time in his life. If that was not enough to cause some anxiety for a teen-ager, the mob scene in Niagara Falls was. The cocky kid from Kitchener counted more than eighty young hockey players at that camp — the best teen-age players from throughout Canada — and his spirits sank. It was like a tap on the shoulder when you are escaping from a store with a dozen phonograph records under your jacket, because, just three weeks hence, when training camp would be over, only twenty of those players would remain in Niagara, and some of the guys in camp had already been with the Flyers for a year or two.

The pressure was intense and severe, because Junior A was just a long slap shot from the majors, and everyone of those young men in that camp was chasing the same dream.

"Give it your best shot," Goldy's parents had told him when he want away, and this would keep him going. He was either too proud or too stubborn to let them down, and even though he had nagging doubts about his ability, he kept telling himself, "I'm going to make this club and that's all there is to it." Still, the doubts served a positive purpose in that they drove him to greater efforts.

If he saw that someone was going to beat him in a skating drill, he just bore down harder. He pushed himself so hard that he would get cramps and burning sensations in his stomach, but he did not mind this discomfort as much as he did getting beat on the ice.

Niagara Falls may be great for honeymooners and people who like to ride barrels over the precipice, but for a seventeen-year-old kid with stars in his eyes and a hockey stick in his hand the glamour of the place wore thin in a hurry.

Those others could come and go as they please, but a Junior A player lives by a strict set of rules, and if he doesn't, then he's packed off for home in a hurry. At least that's the way it was in Niagara. There was a man there — he's still there — by the name of Hap Emms, and he put more boys into professional hockey than anyone anywhere. This he did with discipline and determination. He would drive those young men as they had never been driven before.

That he was a firm disciplinarian was due to the fact that he was mother and father to twenty teen-age boys, most of them away from home for the first time, at an age when the maturity of the body had clearly outdistanced that of the mind.

By coincidence, Hap Emms' greatest rival in the coaching ranks those days was the same Mr. Wren Blair who had built the Whitby Dunlops into a famous amateur hockey machine, but who was then coaching Oshawa, a Junior A team that, like Niagara, was affiliated with the Boston Bruins.

It was ironical that while it was Emms who taught Goldy how to play hockey as it should be played, it would be Blair who ultimately tormented the talent out of the big blonde.

Goldy's first encounter on the ice with Hap was a short exchange.

"You can't skate," said Emms.

"What do you mean I can't skate?" asked the irritated Goldy.

"I'm going to teach you how to skate."

He did. It took time. When practice was over for the other kids, Emms kept Goldy on the ice, teaching him to flex his knees and stride, stride, stride. He had been too stiff in the legs and was not developing the momentum for those streaking rushes down the right side that one day would be his hallmark. Coming in crouched, he also developed better balance against the crunching checks from big, strong defensemen.

Goldy would not become the fastest skater in hockey. There would always be faster ones, guys like Cournoyer of Montreal, or Orr, or the North Stars' Danny Grant, but Goldy was plenty fast. And when he started adding muscle to his 6-1 frame, he looked fast, because there was a lot more of him steaming across the blue line with those long strides.

The early days of that first training camp in Niagara were depressing to Goldy. When the players took to the ice, they would be positioned in three long lines, left wingers on the left, centers in the middle, right wingers on the right, and the first man in each line would make a rush, then the next and the next. Goldy was one of fifteen players on right wing, and out of these, only three or four would be retained.

On the second day of camp the first cuts were made and the youngsters crowded around the bulletin board to see their fate. If it were the first time many of them had been away from home, it was also the first time they did not want to return there. Few, if any, would be invited back next year, because there would be a whole new crop of kids coming out of the midget leagues across Canada and looking for glory. It was now, or never. One good shot, and then . . .

Goldy made the Flyers, and for this he was rewarded with a contract that required several hours of hard practice every day, a lot of homework (until he dropped out of school in his third year there), long bus trips in the night, and $22.50 per week, about $20 of which went for board and room, clothing and other necessities. Sometimes he did not have enough left over for a tube of toothpaste. Anyway, that was one necessity that would become less so as time went on. Anything he could not afford, he just looked at.

When he ran into hard times and really needed something, he'd call back home to Kitchener and tell his mother, "Hey, mum, could you spare a few bucks?"

They always sent him what they could. To Goldy it was like receiving a CARE package.

If times were tough, that was the way it was supposed to be, because Junior A hockey was the equivalent of pre-med school for a doctor, or the apprenticeship system for a carpenter, or a plumber, or a brick layer. You did not get to the top without first suffering a little during the learning process on the way up.

Hap Emms had a strict set of rules. A player caught smoking was fined, and taking a drink meant automatic release. There was little or no bending of the rules. Even the food they ate was dictated by Mr. Hap Emms. They did not eat pastry, hot dogs, pizza and similar food.

All of the Junior A players who were away from their home town lived in boarding houses, and management even sent a list of approved foods to the landlady. This included a lot of meat — chicken, roasts and steak — and fruits and vegetables.

Goldy and his roommates used to sneak a pizza now and then, and their stealth in this avoided detection.

But one night when they went out to watch a Junior B game, Goldy drifted over to the snack stand and ordered a hot dog. He had not had one for a long time, and the temptation had become too great. He opened his mouth to take the first bite, but a tap on the shoulder made him swing around in mid-bite.

"Mr. Goldsworthy, that will cost you $10.20," said Hap Emms, who assessed fines instantly upon the scene of the offense.

"What's the twenty cents for?" asked Goldy.

"That's for the cost of the hot dog."

Just as that first training camp was winding up, school was starting, and the routine would change after that. There was no direct relationship between the schools and the hockey system, but all of the Flyers were expected to handle both.

Goldy had to be up at 8 o'clock to eat and walk the half mile to school in time for 9 o'clock classes. On days the Flyers did not have a game, there would be two hours of practice after school. Evenings were supposed to be devoted to homework, but he roomed with three other players. If one of them wanted to study, the others made so much noise that he gave up.

Anyway, they found the movies more interesting than school work, and spent many evenings in the theaters. A lot of the time the people operating the theater would let them in free, knowing they didn't have much money. On other nights they spent hours in a pool hall, trying to hustle a few extra bucks to take care of their cleaning bills.

Hap Emms' rules specified that his players were to wear clean and pressed slacks and shirts, a rather tall order for a bunch of teen-age kids living in rooming houses. Sometimes Goldy would press his shirt around the collar and down the front a ways, then wear a sweater over it. Underneath the shirt was all wrinkled.

He was not nearly as handy with an iron as with a hockey stick. Once after he had pressed and put on a pair of slacks, his roommate looked at the variety of pleats in the trousers and said, "What are you wearing, a skirt?"

While his money held out, Goldy ate lunch at the school cafeteria, because over one particular period of time when he was without funds his landlady sent a bag lunch along with him, and he had to eat ham sandwiches for a couple of weeks in a row.

The Flyers played a 54-game schedule, which took them on many long road trips. They would travel by bus to towns as much as 200 miles away, and it would be 3 or 4 a.m. before they returned home. Still, they were expected in school at 9 a.m., because the educators made no exceptions for hockey players. They wanted 100 per cent all the time, just as the hockey people did. Some guys could give it to both. Goldy could not.

He had developed his own philosophy on how to achieve success, but he could not apply it to school. For this he would not make any excuses. Goldy simply was in love with hockey, and he approached the game with what he called the "Three D's," meaning desire, dedication and determination.

Many years later he would reflect on this philosophy with some regret that he had not applied it to education: "If I had worked on that in school, I would have done well there, but I didn't. On the ice I had the desire because I had the ability, and I had the determination that nobody was going to beat me. The dedication was to the club and the sweater I was wearing. This all ties in with what you want, and I think it's why I made it to the NHL.

"Sometimes I'm sorry I didn't apply all that to school. But that was my own fault."

Those long bus trips were not entirely a loss in terms of education. Goldy learned how to play cribbage and poker, though he didn't play for money because no one had much of it. Instead, they played for a bunch of IOU's.

If he was not getting rich at Niagara Falls, Goldy was absorbing a wealth of hockey knowledge under Hap Emms. This was beginning to make an impact on the muscular winger, because he was developing as one of the best performers on a very good Flyer team.

He was also filling out his lean frame. Weight lifting and other body building exercises were beginning to add muscle where there had been only skin and bones before. The skinny kid was becoming a big hockey player, but losing none of his speed. He grew from a hard 140 pounds to a solid 175. But his style of play remained the same, this being a kind of chip-on-the-shoulder, hell-bent for trouble style that got him penalties in great bunches. But it did not hurt the team so much in those days, because all of the youngsters in that league were going through the learning process and mistakes were easier to cover up. Besides, Hap Emms' system was designed to get everybody pulling together in a co-ordinated movement, so that when one of them did make a mistake, the others minimized it with systematic team play.

Goldy had a tooth knocked out that first year, and many more would follow in succeeding years. That was a routine thing.

At the end of that first year the Flyers went to the finals of the Memorial Cup playoffs, the Junior A equivalent of the Stanley Cup series, but were beaten by Edmonton in six games.

Goldy didn't go home to spend the summer after that. He got a job with a soft drink company, throwing cases of pop around all day. During the peak of the season, he worked from early morning until 10 or 11 o'clock at night, and this kept him in excellent condition for the start of the second season. Occasionally he hitchhiked the 90 miles home to check up on old friendships, but his heart was not with the Falcons any more. If recognition was what he was looking for, this he got in Niagara, because the Flyers usually played to a full house of 4,000 persons. And Goldy, because of his battering style and his short temper, was becoming a hero or anti-hero with the Flyer partisans.

That second year at Niagara would be Goldy's last one in school. He could see that it was not in his nature to give 100 per cent to both school and hockey, and that doing both was hurting both. He decided to give everything he had to hockey, knowing that if he fell by the wayside he would have no kind of career training to fall back on.

It was not an unexpected decision from a teen-age kid whose whole life seemed to be channelled toward a career in professional hockey. There was simply nothing else that counted at that stage.

Niagara Falls existed for the purpose of developing major league hockey players. Hap Emms remained for the same reason. Goldy had gone there for the same reason, and his dedication to his goal was complete and unbending. Just as he had when he was a child, he would spend Saturday night in front of a television set watching Hockey Night in Canada, if the Flyers weren't in action on Saturday, and many of those stars and super stars who glided across the face of the screen had, only a few years previously, played Junior A hockey. Many of them had come out of Niagara.

On some occasions when the Flyers traveled by train, they would end up in the same depot with one of the NHL teams that were doing some train travel in those days. Goldy once saw Bobby Hull, the sensation of the NHL, and other Black Hawks like Moose Vasko and Doug Mohns, in one of those train depots, and even though he dreamed those dreams, he could not visualize that someday he would be sent out to play head to head with the great Hull, or that he would be taking lead passes from the slick Mohns to start a scoring play or playing with Vasko on the Stars' original team.

One of Goldy's teammates and closest friends in those days at Niagara Falls was a free spirit by the name of Derek Sanderson, who would go on to play with the mighty Bruins and become such a controversial player that he would have his face on the cover of Life magazine.

Hap Emms again took his Flyers to the Memorial Cup playoffs that second year Goldy was there, but this time they were eliminated by the Toronto Marlboros. It was after this season that Goldy dropped out of school to work full time at hockey.

Some players who were every bit as good, if not better than Goldy in those days, would not make it to the big time because they were forever working on their strengths. Goldy worked on his weaknesses, not all, but most of them. He practiced endlessly on his stick handling, breaking into holes, taking the puck off the tricky boards and perfecting his shot. One weakness, his greatest, he was not mentally prepared to cope with at that young age: his temper would continue to plague him.

In his third year at Niagara, Goldy and the Flyers once again went to the Memorial Cup playoffs, and this time they came home with the trophy symbolic of the greatest Junior A team in all of Canada.

Goldy made one trip without the Flyers that third season.

"How would you like to spend a weekend in Boston?" asked Hap Emms one day in practice.

"Doing what?" asked Goldy.

"Playing with the Bruins."

"You've got to be kidding!"

"They want you for the weekend," said Hap.

Goldy was just nineteen when he skated out onto the ice at Boston Gardens. He wasn't the youngest player ever in the NHL, but he probably was right up there with the most nervous of them.

The Bruins, then the doormat of the NHL, were looking for help wherever they could get it, and the furious young man on the right side of the Niagara attack might inject some spirit into their ranks.

The brush with fame was fleeting and discouraging. Goldy played only briefly and unspectacularly in the two weekend games, with Boston taking a thrashing in both.

"How was it?" asked Hap, when Goldy arrived back in Niagara.

"Next time I'm bringing my own puck. They wouldn't let me get close to the one they were playing with."

Hockey people have always kept detailed reports on the abilities of Junior A players, and Goldy's dossier as he finished his playing days at Niagara was filled with positive assessments of his talent. But there was that one disturbing thing that balanced the reports and caused hockey management to look upon him with doubt and skepticism: he was a hothead who, rubbed the wrong way, was prone to ignite a brawl as though he were spearheading the charge in a gang war off in the gravel pits of Kitchener. Trouble seemed to follow him. Or perhaps it was the child of his own inner turmoil.

Something very important happened there in Niagara Falls that was not directly related to his hockey career, but it would influence it later. During the summer when he was throwing pop cases around, he was also playing softball for a local team. It was at one of those softball games that Goldy met June Ness. She was petite and pretty, with big round eyes and dark hair. She could barely reach to his shoulders, standing on her toes.

June's brother was coach of the softball team Goldy played for. One night, another brother was the umpire behind the plate, and a third was the umpire on the bases. Whether they objected to the blonde young man going out with their sister, or whether it was just coincidence, a big argument erupted on the diamond that night. Goldy was on base — a rare occurrence — and June's brother called him out for leaving the base before the ball crossed the plate.

June was not much impressed with Goldy's prowess on the softball field. She once assessed his performance this way: "He stunk. He couldn't play ball. Half the time he was looking up in the stands and taking wild swings but never hitting anything. I don't know if he was watching me, but he was watching somebody."

Softball abilities aside, June liked Goldy. But she thought he was a little peculiar about some things, especially in the matter of dress. Even during extremely hot days of the summer he would wear a sweater over his shirt, causing him to perspire freely. She did not know that underneath that sweater his shirt, the part of it not showing, was a mass of wrinkles. Even romance could not inspire him to strive for proficiency over the ironing board.

Goldy and June dated a lot that summer, and two years later they would be married.

So it worked out that Niagara Falls was not necessarily a place of unrelenting contradictions: matrimony and mayhem were compatible for some.

Chapter IV

War Drums in Oklahoma

Harry Sinden, coach of the Oklahoma City Blazers, settled into the comfortable chair at a table in the Tenth Inning cocktail lounge, and ordered refreshments for his wife and the other couple accompanying them. The waitress returned with the cocktails, and as Sinden lifted his glass he looked up at the combo on the stage nearby. It was a black combo, five players, with a lot of talent. Only this time, to Sinden's dismay, there were only four black faces and one very white one up on that stage. Goldy, his blonde hair flying, was beating the drums with enthusiasm, if not the greatest rhythm.

Sinden choked on his drink, got up and led his group out, the ice still tinkling in their unfinished cocktails as they went through the door. Goldy drummed on.

"What were you doing in that combo last night!" Sinden demanded, when he confronted his big right winger the next day.

"Playing the drums," said Goldy. He had become friends with the musicians and had asked to sit in for one set on the drums.

"You were lousy. That will be a $200 fine."

Hockey players, no matter how unruly their conduct on the ice, are expected to be models of good manners and proper behavior when out in public.

Goldy wasn't a bad drummer, having taken up the instrument in his late teens and spending a lot of time practicing. Ultimately the $200 would be returned to him, unlike other fine money he lost in Oklahoma City.

Goldy had come to Oklahoma following his last year at Niagara. Some guys were more fortunate, being plucked right out of the Junior A ranks and injected into the majors when they reached twenty years of age. Only a few years ago there was no age restriction, but few kids were ready for the NHL before twenty. There were exceptions, like Bobby Orr. Orr was born ready, even though he was eighteen before the Boston Bruins took him.

The wheel of fortune spins an erratic path. When Bobby Orr was fourteen, he was signed into the Bruins' farm system by Wren Blair. The Bird, with his intense dislike of losing, was not about to give up this hot young prospect.

When Blair signed Orr the contract carried a stipulation: Bobby was to play Junior A hockey for The Bird. This rankled Hap Emms, because the way this thing was set up, Emms normally got the pick of the twenty players he wanted for his Niagara team, and the Oshawa club, also in the Bruin organization and also Junior A, got the leftovers. Bobby Orr was not built to be a leftover. But Blair had him on his

Oshawa team, and even though the other nineteen players may have been leftovers, Oshawa usually played Niagara Falls to a standoff.

The games were brutal, because the players on both teams were battling for the same prize: their name on the program at Boston Gardens.

Blair had little trouble getting his team ready for a game with the Flyers. He'd strut into the dressing room before game time and say: "Those guys are out to get you and take your job with Boston. Are you going to let them do it?"

"Like hell!" was the cry that came back. But Blair, when Niagara was playing elsewhere, would pull for the Flyers. They were in the Bruin family, too.

In those days Goldy was one of the top players for the Flyers, and Blair always put his toughest checker on him. Usually it was Wayne Cashman. Blair took Cashman aside before the game and said, "Your job is to be as superior a hockey player for us as Goldy is for them. Let's see what you can do about it."

Oshawa had the baby-faced Orr, Cashman and Danny O'Shea, and Niagara had Goldy, Derek Sanderson and Bernie Parent, and every game was a massacre because of the competition for a spot with the Bruins.

In one of those games Goldy had gotten the only penalty shots of his career. He was so nervous when he skated in on the goalie all alone that he shot the puck over the top of the net. The referee, noticing that young Orr was standing over the center line in violation of the rules, awarded Goldy a second penalty shot. His nerves frazzled by the first experience, this time Goldy missed an open corner of the net by firing a shot twenty feet wide of the goal.

With his leftovers and the magnificent young Orr, Blair's Oshawa team put Niagara out of the playoffs in The Bird's fourth year. Goldy was gone then.

He spent the summer of his third year at Niagara working for the soft drink company and dating June and trying to prepare himself mentally for a very important training camp that fall.

In September Goldy packed his gear, said his goodbyes to June and Niagara Falls, and drove off to London, Ontario, where the Boston Bruins were opening camp. Even though the Bruins had been dead last in the NHL the previous year, there were a lot of fine hockey players in London. Goldy worked hard at that training camp and made an impression on the Bruin management. He survived all the cuts made there and was still on the roster when the Bruins broke camp and headed to Beantown to complete the exhibition season. There the final cuts were made, and Goldy lingered until the end. He was the last man dropped. The Bruins decided he could use more seasoning in the minors with their Oklahoma City farm team in the Central Professional Hockey League.

Oklahoma City was approximately a world and a half away from Boston for a twenty-year-old kid who had once skated with the Bruins in Boston Gardens. But if Goldy was discouraged, he was too busy trying to survive in Oklahoma City to give much time to self pity.

The people in that southern climate had not been exposed to the game of hockey very long, and they looked upon it as a hybrid sport combining boxing, wrestling and ice skating, with a liberal amount of audience participation. It was the kind of environment in which Goldy thrived, having not long been out of the gravel pits of Kitchener. Goldy became a folk hero in Oklahoma City. Tulsa was something else. Once they sent the cops after him with handcuffs in Tulsa.

The rivalry between the two teams was bitter beyond any plausible explanation. Whenever they met, be it in Oklahoma City or Tulsa, they would play to a full house. Tulsa people would come to Oklahoma City to cheer their warriors and taunt the Blazers, and on one of these occasions a fan jumped out onto the ice with two policemen in hot pursuit, just as Goldy was skating to the bench. The man trotted along the boards behind the seething winger, cursing him and making childish noises.

Goldy spun around and threw an uppercut that caught the boisterous individual mid-cheek, sending him sailing back into the arms of the advancing police.

In a game at Tulsa a brawl erupted on the ice, and when it was finally brought under control, the cops were there with the irons and hauled Goldy away to the lockup. The case against him was dismissed.

Tempers were always at the boiling point in those minor league games because everyone down there was trying to get to the top. You would not make it if you could be intimidated. The Blazers could not be intimidated. They had a lot of good, tough hockey players who one day would fight their way to the big time, guys like Gerry Cheevers, Bernie Parent, Doug Favell, Dallas Smith, Dave Woodley, Wayne Cashman, Terry Crisp and Jean-Paul Parise.

Parise and Goldy became good friends, much in the same way that soldiers fighting side by side in the trenches develop a strong bond.

One night a delegation of more than fifty rabid fans from Tulsa had come to Oklahoma City to needle the Blazers, and through some quirk of fate they were seated in the section right behind the Blazers' bench. There they proceeded to throw drinks onto the players, starting a free-for-all. Goldy spotted one particularly hostile fan who had taunted the team in previous engagements, and he climbed up over the boards in back of the bench and onto the seats. He moved stealthily toward the tormentor, who did not see Goldy coming. As Goldy cocked his arm, a hand clasped his shoulder.

"Nope, I want him," said J.P. Parise.

"Like heck, I want him," said Goldy.

"You can have him next time," said J.P., a dark, tough Frenchman.

J.P. delivered a blow that stunned the heckler into silence.

Meanwhile, the brawl had progressed onto the ice, where there was a great squirming pile of players and spectators. A young man, later identified as an all-state wrestling champ from Oklahoma City, climbed up on top of the boards and dove right into the pile. As he went to work, bodies came flying out of the pileup in all directions.

A few times during that first season in the minors Goldy was called up to Boston. In his very first game up there he scored his first NHL goal. But in all he was only up for thirteen games, not enough to set the Bruins on fire.

The reports on him then, as before, were that he could be NHL caliber if he only realized his potential and stayed out of trouble.

Some really serious trouble of a different nature awaited him upon his return to Oklahoma City from one of those trips up to the big time. Ironically enough, it was in a game against arch-rival Tulsa that Goldy took a hard check into the goal post, tearing the cartilage and ligaments in his right knee and leg.

The injury required surgery, and Goldy would sit out the second half of the season as well as the championship playoffs.

The Blazers won the playoffs without him, beating out a loaded St. Louis team that had the likes of Dennis Hull, Pat Stapleton, Chico Maki, Fred Stanfield and John Miszuk.

Back in Niagara Falls, June had not heard from Goldy after he had left that previous summer, but in February she received a telephone call from Bill's mother in Kitchener.

"June, Bill is going to have a knee operation in Niagara Falls this month; will you visit with him while he is there?"

He was there just long enough for two operations, the second one performed because the first had not been successful in repairing the badly-damaged knee. After the two weeks he was gone again, driving back to Oklahoma City to be with the Blazers through the finish of the season.

That summer, at the end of his first year in the minors, Goldy went back to Niagara Falls to once again work for the soft drink company he had spent previous summers with. It was then that he and June decided to marry, but they chose to wait until the next hockey season was over. Only then would they know if the injured leg would threaten Goldy's career.

Despite warnings that the knee and leg would be weak, and that only constant exercise would bring it back to normal, Goldy did not give the limb a test until the start of training camp. He was young and strong and stubborn, and was convinced that if he could walk, he could skate.

When he got to camp he could barely skate. The leg was so weak he could not lift a five-pound weight with it. For the next few weeks he went on a crash program to bring it back. He rode a bicycle exercise machine the equivalent of forty to fifty miles every day, and lifted weights, gradually increasing the amount of weight the leg could lift. By the start of the season, his injured leg was as strong as the other.

If Goldy had not set the NHL on fire in his thirteen games at Boston the previous year, he would cause some slow burns in Oklahoma this one. For one thing, even with the bad leg and not knowing how it would affect his play, he was a holdout. When he finally came to terms he was late getting to camp, and the management hung a brief suspension on him.

That was only the beginning of a troublesome season. In hockey there are guys who are known as "home" players, and others as "road" players. Some who play very well before the partisan home crowd do not do well on foreign ice where the going is always tougher. Others get higher when they are in the enemy camp, but don't do nearly as well at home. Goldy liked to play anywhere, and was particularly effective on the road. During one stretch of five road games in that second season at Oklahoma City he had scored four goals and three assists for seven points.

Despite the fact that he was in the middle of a hot streak, when the team returned home he sat out most of the next two games while the "home" players were getting most of the ice time. In an impulsive fit of anger, he left the arena without permission.

"Get me out of here. I want to play hockey," he said as he was leaving.

They did, but only after a flurry of activity that included an indefinite suspension of the winger.

The day following his abrupt departure from the ice, Goldy discussed his action with a newspaper reporter.

"I made a bad play. I had been scoring well and I couldn't stand being held out of the game. I know I can play hockey, but I know I've got to curb my temper. It's been against me all the time and I'm trying to control it. I will, if they'll let me stay here and play. I've solved the problem with my leg, and I'm sure I can solve the other one. What I want is a chance."

He got the chance, elsewhere, partly because there was too much potential there to give up on him, and perhaps because his fate was determined by the general manager of the parent Boston Bruins. At that time it was Hap Emms, who was not about to toss away all those post-practice hours he had devoted to teaching Goldy how to skate at Niagara.

The suspension was lifted and Goldy was shipped off to Buffalo. He would not see the Central Hockey League again, but for a very brief and bitter visit a couple of years later.

Buffalo was good for Goldy, for two reasons: he could see June more often, and he played a lot both at home and on the road. He became a fury on the right side of the Buffalo attack, and in 21 games scored 10 goals and 11 assists.

Over at Boston the Bruins were having a tough time getting that kind of scoring as a team. Coach Harry Sinden's club was at the bottom of the heap, and his small forward lines had been getting pushed around all season. Even if he had not thought too highly of Goldy's drumming ability at Oklahoma City the year before, Sinden respected the winger's hockey talent.

"He can skate and he can score," said the Bruin coach. "He gives us a little size up front and he'll hit a few guys. He's not afraid to check. I don't know if he can fight, but I don't care. Jean Beliveau can't fight, but he's a great hockey player."

Goldy did not go to Boston to fight. He never intended to. He wanted only to play hockey, and that he played it in the only way he knew how — intense and roughshod — caused him some grief, because the opposition, like the management of the Bruin organization, knew he was a tempestuous young man given to retaliation when someone lashed out at him.

Later, he reflected upon those turbulent early days in the big time:

"I never really classified myself as a bad guy, or let's say a tough guy, and I didn't think I was the world's greatest fighter. If I were, I wouldn't be on the ice; I'd be in the ring. But Boston always taught us to play the body. When we were young they taught us this. They like to have you hit, to mix it up. That's fine, and it didn't hurt the club too much in the Junior ranks if you got 200 minutes in penalties.

"But as time went on and I got in the pros, maybe I was retaliating too much. You know, one of the first things they do up there in the majors is come after you hard to see if they can intimidate you or if you will retaliate. This was the best league I could ever play in, and I was determined not to lose my job by getting run off the ice. Consequently I was hurting the club with too many penalty minutes.

"I never went looking for a fight, but I guess I have always had my share of them. And it seems as though I was always on the bottom. That's bad, because when you're on the bottom you have to fight harder to get out."

Despite the enthusiastic endorsements from Sinden and the local press, Goldy did little to lift the Bruins out of their depression. He spent most of the time on the bench. And the future did not look promising, because Boston was developing a stable of great hockey talent that in a few years would be heralded as one of the greatest hockey teams of modern history. There was the incredible young Orr, and Phil Esposito and Johnny Bucyk and Derek Sanderson (with whom Goldy had become close friends at Niagara Falls), and John McKenzie, and some others just on the threshold of becoming great players.

There was also Tommy Williams, one of the few American-born players who had ever developed the ability to skate with the Canadians. And even that ability was due in a large measure to an apprenticeship in the Canadian hockey mills.

Goldy and Williams built a close relationship in the short time they were together at Boston, and later they would be reunited to form two-thirds of a forward line that established a scoring record for expansion league hockey teams. Their friendship was due, perhaps, to a certain mutual affinity for trouble: Goldy's on the ice, and Tommy's off.

They would have another thing in common: the lives of both would be touched by the stern and stormy Mr. Wren Blair. Few hockey players whose lives have been touched by The Bird would likely forget the experience.

After those many years of effort to get to Boston, Goldy would become dispensible in the historic expansion draft for the 1967-68 season. It might have been the fact that there was too much other really good hockey talent to protect in the draft. Or it might have been his temper. Every time Goldy barreled over the boards onto the ice at Boston Gardens, it was like the Tea Party all over again.

The Bruins were not looking to start a revolution. All they wanted was Lord Stanley's Cup.

Goldy was in a Bruin uniform when the season ended, but he did not expect to be back the following year. The draft was coming up in the summer of 1967, and he had no illusions that he would be protected. This did not concern him. He was looking forward to the opportunity to go with an expansion team where he would get a better shot at proving himself.

But first, he was looking forward to matrimony He and June had planned to be married after the season, and on April 29 they said their vows in St. Stephens Lutheran Church in Kitchener. It was a small wedding, consisting only of members of the two families. Goldy's brother, Ken, came home on leave from the RCAF to serve as best man. None of the close friends Goldy had made in hockey was there, because they were still in Oklahoma City. He had not been with Buffalo or the Bruins long enough to establish close friendships.

The young couple took a two-week honeymoon trip, driving down to Boston and then to Cape Cod where they saw the Kennedy estate, then to upper New York state for a stay at Lake Placid. From there they drove to Montreal to see Expo 67 from a bridge, having no money to take in the exposition. Finally, they drove to Ottawa where Goldy's brother was stationed.

They went back to Niagara Falls, June's home, and rented a small furnished apartment in the basement of a brick house. It cost them $20 a week,

which left them with little money to buy more fur-
nishings. That didn't matter much, because the
future was uncertain, with the draft coming up that
June.

What little furniture the apartment did have
would have delighted an antique furniture dealer.
The ancient bed had an errant spring that kept
popping through the mattress at approximately mid-
bed, and every so often they had to push it back
down and pull the stuffing over it. The kitchen had
an old wooden table with one leg shorter than the
others, and two time-worn wooden chairs.

The living room of the apartment was the
showplace, containing a lamp and a sofa with a big
hump in the middle.

It was, in short, a typical first home for a young
married couple without any money.

Even so, they were fortunate in getting what they
did, because for most apartments around there they
would have to sign a six-month or one-year lease.
They had no idea where they would be in six months,
but it was not going to be Niagara Falls.

June worked as a secretary for a consulting
engineers' firm while Goldy went back on the job at
the soft drink place. They budgeted their incomes
carefully, since Goldy would need funds to get to
training camp, wherever that might be.

On that summer day in 1967 when the NHL draft
was taking place, Goldy and June sat by the radio
and waited for the news. Throughout the day the
Canadian radio stations would make up-to-the-
minute reports on the progress of the draft.

"Minnesota picked Bill Goldsworthy on the 9th round," the radio said.

Goldy looked at June. "Where's Minnesota?"

A few days later a letter arrived, telling him he was now the property of the Minnesota North Stars, and that he was to report to training camp at Haliburton, Ontario that fall.

Goldy would go to Minnesota only a handful of years away from those rough and tumble days in Kitchener, and he would go as a different person in many respects. Where once he had been footloose and irresponsible, he was beginning to mature with the responsibilities of marriage.

"Marriage makes the difference for most guys as it did for me," he said later. "Suddenly, instead of swinging carefree through life, you have a wife and you're setting up a home. For once you're thinking in terms of the future. It makes you see you have responsibilities. All of a sudden you have a reason to do well and build a good life for more than just a little glory."

June would stay in Niagara with her parents that fall when Goldy went off to Haliburton and his first encounter with a gentleman called The Bird.

Chapter V

"The Bird"

"Good Lord," said Wren Blair, looking at his $2 million worth of playing personnel, "just look at this mess. This is supposed to be a major league hockey team. There are only four guys on this list that are major league players. Your job and mine is to unload the other 16 just as fast as we can, any way we can. I'll trade 10-for-one if I have to."

Blair and his scouting staff of the new Minnesota North Star organization had just finished making their player selections in the expansion draft of 1967, and had gathered in his hotel suite to assess what they had obtained for the mere price of $100,000 per man.

Later someone would ask The Bird: "Well, why did you pick the guys if they weren't major league caliber?"

"Because that's all we had to choose from!" The Bird snapped back.

They studied and re-studied that roster of players in that hotel suite, but the talk always drifted back to the same conclusion: they had gained a pretty promising goalie, the lanky Cesare Maniago, as their first pick in the goaltender draft, and they had a couple of pretty fair wings and one solid defenseman. But, on paper, they did not have enough proven talent for one line, much less the three or four they would need that season.

"When we started that first year — the team we had — it was just brutal," said Blair. "If you had that team and said to a coach, 'Here's your team,' he would throw up his hands and swear.

"Building an NHL team from the formula given us at expansion time was a real grind. It still is. It was like the neighborhood bully coming down the street and saying, 'Okay, let's choose up sides and play a game. I'm going to take the first 11 guys, now you can have one.' You know what the outcome of that game will be in any neighborhood in North America."

At one time during the course of the draft selection Blair went up to Clarence Campbell, president of the NHL, and said, "We have eighteen players and we pass. We don't want any more."

"You have to take twenty," Campbell said.

They took twenty, which only meant they would have two more players to trade away later. Blair did not unload sixteen players from that original roster as promised. He peddled eighteen of them over the next four years, and along the way traded some guys he had obtained for some of the original twenty.

Even with that original cast of misfits, unknowns and castoffs, The Bird put together a National Hockey League team that came within one game of going to the finals of the Stanley Cup playoffs, partly on the strength of a sensational performance by a blonde kid out of Kitchener, Ontario, who Blair drove mercilessly at times.

The first year success of the North Stars was, by the standards of those trying times, nothing short of phenomenal. Their accomplishments on the ice were exceeded in drama only by the contortions that led to the formation of the North star organization.

When the NHL had made its decision to expand from six to twelve teams, the competition was fierce for the six new franchises. Among those putting in bids were the sister cities of Minneapolis and St. Paul, which, by the grace of God, are largely separated by the Mississippi River. This great natural barrier has prevented many war-like acts from breaking into open violence. The sisters do not get along very well. They bickered over a professional baseball franchise, and when an armistice was forged, the Minnesota Twins were settled in Bloomington, Minnesota, a suburb consisting primarily of bedrooms and schools.

They haggled over a professional football franchise, and the Minnesota Vikings also ended up in Bloomington. The bedroom community of Bloomington had become the demilitarized zone for the warring sisters.

Having learned nothing from these two er-periences, Minneapolis and St. Paul bickered anew over a hockey franchise. There was never any question of them getting two franchises; one would have been a big fat prize.

"I remember that February day in 1966 when the applications for the Minnesota franchise were made," said NHL President Campbell. "In my wildest dreams I could not visualize that a franchise would come out of the chaos surrounding the Minnesota bid."

The Twin Cities people had made their presentations at the St. Regis Hotel in New York City.

"Philadelphia had just made a neat and orderly application," Campbell said, "and then the Minnesota groups came forth, bickering among themselves in an atmosphere of hostility that actually approached hatred. Finally they left the room and I said to myself, 'That's the last I'll ever see of them. There's no way they can ever get together.'"

It was not an easy truce this time, but when it was ultimately arranged, the Minnesota North Stars would be settled in the DMZ of Bloomington.

That Minnesota got a franchise at all was due in large measure to a 36-year-old Minneapolis attorney and a radio-television executive who had been part owners of the Minneapolis Bruin hockey team in the Boston chain.

Walter Bush, the attorney, who would become president of the North Star organization, had long been active in amateur hockey, once serving as manager of the U.S. Olympic team. Gordon Ritz, who was to become Minnesota's representative on the NHL Board of Governors, also had an active interest in hockey.

These two, plus Robert McNulty, a Twin Cities area developer, had partially financed the Minneapolis Bruins in the Central Hockey League during the 1963-64 and 1964-65 seasons, and this proved to be a $180,000 loser over the two years.

As early as 1965 there were rumors abroad that the NHL was planning to expand, and Bush wrote President Clarence Campbell that a group of Twin Cities people was interested in a franchise. Throughout the summer of 1965 the eight members of a syndicate organized by Bush and Ritz explored various ways of remodeling and expanding the Hippodrome at the Minnesota State Fairgrounds, to meet the minimum seating requirement of 12,500.

The expenditure of time and effort on this plan proved fruitless, when a consultant sent out by the NHL said it was not feasible. This disturbing news reached the syndicate members late in 1965, with the date for expansion applications coming up in early 1966.

No one in the syndicate was interested in investing in a new building, which would cost several million dollars.

The group then approached the City of St. Paul about the possibility of remodelling the St. Paul Auditorium for their use. This proposal progressed to the stage where rental agreements were worked out, and the syndicate had been assured that the expansion of the facility would not require a referendum vote. This was critical to the issue, since the NHL requirements specified that an immediate, long-term lease would be needed.

Only one week prior to the New York meeting, the City of St. Paul was informed by a consultant it had retained that a referendum vote would be required.

The syndicate's dream had collapsed.

It was then that a second group of eight men, four each from Minneapolis and St. Paul, announced they would bid for a franchise. The two groups met in advance of the New York meeting, but could reach no accord. Both groups sent representatives to New York. There they argued for two days before reaching a compromise of sorts, whereby Bush's group would go before the Board of Governors and push for the St. Paul Auditorium, in spite of the need for a referendum. The Bush people would also make ten per cent ownership of the franchise available to the second syndicate.

Try as they did, they could not get the Board of Governors to change its collective mind about the Auditorium.

"Could we have an hour's recess to discuss this situation?" asked Bush.

"Absolutely not," said one of the governors, "we'll give you five minutes."

Bush, Ritz and Bob Ridder, another radio-television executive and a member of the syndicate, huddled outside the conference room. They had but two choices left to them: drop the bid completely, or promise a new building for which they had no plans, no financing or no property to put it on.

They went back in and promised to have a new building ready for play by the start of the 1967-68 season.

On February 9 of 1966, one of the six new franchises was awarded to the Twin Cities, even though there was no building, the area had the

PIED PIPER OF HALIBURTON — At Haliburton Hockey Haven, a hockey school in Ontario, Goldy is often called the "Pied Piper of Haliburton," because of his rapport with youngsters and excellent knowledge of the game. The North Star winger is an instructor at Haliburton during the off season. Here he discusses the proper curve of a stick.

TOMMY WILLIAMS, one of the few American-born hockey players in the NHL, breaks in front of Gilles Marotte of Los Angeles. A native of Duluth, Minnesota, Tommy was traded by the Stars to California in 1971. The previous year the line of Williams, Goldsworthy and J.P. Parise ranked second in total points in the NHL.

PURSUING BOBBY ORR (what else is new in the NHL?) are North Star Center Jude Drouin, left, and Goldy.

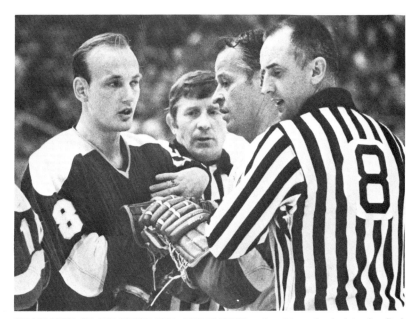

GOLDY PICKS ON CHILDHOOD IDOL GORDY HOWE, an impulsive action he later described as "a bad mistake." Linesmen Pat Shetler, left, and Neil Armstrong separate the two. Howe, to the relief of many opponents, retired shortly before the 1971-72 season.

ONE OF THE TWO REMAINING NORTH STARS of the 1967 expansion team is Goalie Cesare Maniago, here preparing to stop a Detroit Red Wing rush with teammate Tom Reid. Maniago and Goldsworthy are charter members of the Minnesota club which has seen 78 others wear the gold, green and white during the first four years.

THE VIGOR OF YOUTH AND VALUE OF EXPERIENCE — Minnesota's progress as a maturing hockey team is characterized by the youthful vigor of up-and-coming Defenseman Fred Barrett (3), balanced by the experience of two key veterans, Defenseman Ted Harris and Goalie Gump Worsley.

FOILED! Goldy (8) sprawls on the ice at the mouth of Los Angeles' goal. Netminder for the Kings is Wayne Rutledge. Kneeling at left is Bob Wall, L. A. wing.

NHL'S TOP SCORER IN 1970-71 — Phil Esposito, Boston's prolific scoring ace, paused during game at Met.

FUTURE SUPERSTAR? — North Star Center Jude Drouin (16) hustles after puck during a home game with the Red Wings. In his freshman year (1970-71) Jude placed second in voting for the NHL's Calder Trophy, established a rookie record in assists with 52 and played a large role in the goalscoring feats of linemates Danny Grant and Bill Goldsworthy.

FRIENDLY FOES — Fierce competitors on the ice but amiable pals outside the arena, Goldy and Derek Sanderson of Boston attempt to unscramble after collision at the Met.

GO, GO GOLDY! Detroit winger Nick Libett and Bill Goldsworthy pursue puck in Met Sports Center clash.

President Walter Bush, left, and General Manager Wren Blair, whose respective talents and drive led to the founding and shaping of the Minneapolis North Stars, check their personnel roster prior to the start of the 1971-1972 season.

WINNERS AND LOSERS — Montreal Canadiens celebrate after their 3-2 victory to clinch the Stanley Cup semi-finals at the Met in 1971. At right North Stars Tom Reid (20) and Bill Goldsworthy (8) pursue Referee Bill Friday after Ted Hampson's goal was ruled one second late. (Wide World Photos)

ONE SECOND TOO LATE — Goldy argues with Referee Bill Friday after Montreal's 3-2 victory to win the 1971 Stanley Cup semi-final playoff series. Friday disallowed an apparent North Star goal officials said was scored one second after the final buzzer. At left is Minnesota's Ted Hampson who had shot the puck in the nets. (Wide World Photos)

smallest population of all the applicants, had the smallest television market, and had two minor league hockey teams, one in Minneapolis and one in St. Paul, that had flopped financially.

The syndicate spent from February to October of 1966 getting financing for the structure worked out, and in late October construction was started.

It was then less than a year to the start of the 1967 hockey season, and one sage observed that they would have to hire the crew that built the pyramids to get the job done on time.

Though he had never supervised the construction of a pyramid, McNulty, the developer who had been part owner of the Minneapolis Bruins and was a member of the syndicate of eight, saw to it that Met Sports Center did become a reality in time for the opening of that expansion season.

The structure, considered one of the finest hockey houses in the NHL, was rushed to completion by a team that included the Ernest M. Ganley Construction Company of Minneapolis, the general contractor; Bruch and Morrow, Inc., an engineering firm of which one partner was Leigh Morrow, who had coached an amateur hockey team that had beaten out one coached by Walter Bush en route to the U.S. Amateur Hockey Championship years before; and Egan and Sons, Inc., a Minneapolis mechanical-electrical contractor presided over by Cos Egan, who had once played basketball for a championship University of Minnesota team and who might have had some knowledge of pyramid construction since he, himself, was built somewhat like one of those Egyptian monuments turned upside down.

Pattee Architects, Inc., another Minneapolis firm, did the architectural design.

The other members of the original North Star syndicate, in addition to Bush, Ritz, Ridder and McNulty, were Wheelock Whitney, an investment company executive; John Ordway, Jr., president of a St. Paul firm; Harry McNeely, Jr., a trucking executive and one-time state squash champion; and John Driscoll, an officer of a lumber company.

The eight were split evenly between Minneapolis and St. Paul, which made the success of the franchise bid a bigger miracle than the successful completion of the hockey arena for that first season.

It was one thing to have a franchise and quite another to field a respectable hockey team. Savvy as they were about the game, the Minnesota people could not be expected to know the insides of the system that produced the material of which NHL teams are made. Only someone who lived within the system could know where to go for talent.

The Minnesotans went after Wren Blair, then coach and general manager of the Oshawa Junior A team in the Bruin organization, and long successful in amateur hockey.

Bush had known Blair for years, and The Bird had served as general manager for the Minneapolis Bruins, of which Bush was part owner, even though Blair was living in Oshawa in those days.

Sometimes in athletics a coach comes along with such an intense desire to excel that he injects this desire into his players. He is usually demanding and explosive, and because of these qualities evokes either deep respect or anger from those he drives. Often both, though the anger is mostly temporary, coming, as it does, during the heat of the battle.

Wren Blair is that kind of man.

He was a coach that veteran players, once rookies who had felt the sting of his tongue, would come back to years later and say, "I'll bet those guys you've got now don't have it as tough as we did." Then, when they had matured and could reflect back upon those tumultuous times with The Bird, they knew that what he had done to discipline and drive them had helped shape their careers, even if Blair's ways had seemed harsh on them as young men.

Everywhere he went he built winning teams. Their success seemed to be an outgrowth or projection of The Bird's own ego. He simply could not stand to lose, and he could not stand for his players accepting such an unthinkable thought. So they couldn't.

Blair had coached and managed professional, junior and amateur teams in Oshawa, Kingston, Whitby (all in Ontario) and Clinton, N.Y. His genius in finding talent in young hockey players led to the building of one of the greatest amateur hockey teams in the world — the Whitby Dunlops. Blair coached the Dunlops to the 1957-58 Allan Cup Championship, top senior amateur award in Canada. Not satisfied to be the best in Canada, he took the team to the World Amateur Tournament in Oslo, Norway, and came back with that championship, too.

As general manager and coach of the North Stars, Blair would toil long and hard that first year — too long and too hard because it affected his health — to put a team on the ice that would not be ravaged by the existing powerhouses.

His first order of business was to put together a scouting system that could range afar in search of the talent with which to stock the club. He hired as his personal assistant John Mariucci, a craggy-faced former NHL player who was then coaching the U.S. National team.

Harold Cotton was named director of scouting and Ted O'Connor, chief scout. Blair's brother, Gerald, was retained as assistant chief scout. The scouting staff ran up $100,000 in salaries and expenses as they beat the underbrush in the hockey world for prospects. Each carried a tape recorder with which to make first hand observations right at rinkside.

The investment in the talent search was considered money well spent, considering the $100,000 price tag put on each player picked up from existing teams in the player draft.

When the draft was over and Blair and his staff were shedding tears over their $2 million worth of partial-talent, the folks back in Minnesota were conducting a contest to find a name for their team. Of the 1200 entries, 52 suggested the name North Stars, and this won out over such imaginative creations as Norsemen, Voyageurs, Blades, Mustangs, Muskies, Lumberjacks, Mallards, Ospreys, Parjeters, Puckeroos, Tintors, Zips, Go-

Goers and Marauders, this last one probably most descriptive of the team's style of play that first year.

Blair was not content to sit tight with his draftees, and even before that first season started he was dealing for other talent. Among those he acquired from Montreal for cash was center Bill Masterton, who had retired from hockey and was then employed by Honeywell, in the Twin Cities area. Masterton had been an All-America player for Denver University, and had been a standout for Hull-Ottawa in the Eastern Professional Hockey League, and Cleveland of the American Hockey League, before retiring. Masterton would be a central figure in that turbulent, tragic, trying first year of the North Stars, dying after striking his head on the ice in a mid-season game.

True to his word about unloading many of his original draftees for players of NHL caliber, Blair would continue to be an active trader. For this he often came under fire of the local press, which, like the press everywhere, had developed its own stable of experts who knew more about hockey than Wren Blair. In that first year he traded five players off his major league roster for two minor leaguers — J.P. Parise and Milan Marcetta. Later he dealt away the popular Billy Collins to get Jude Drouin, a flying young center who would make a bold bid for Rookie of the Year in 1970-71, and swapped Danny O'Shea, a center, to get Doug Mohns, a defenseman for the Chicago Black Hawks.

Through trades, the Stars picked up a number of good hockey players, and some biting criticism from the press and the North Star partisans. The Bird was not insensitive to this criticism, and at times ruffled his feathers in indignation that his moves in the trade market could be challenged.

"Those people who made all the noise when we traded Collins for Drouin didn't know Drouin from a pumpkin. But I knew who Jude Drouin was. We're paying out $300,000 a year in salaries and expenses for myself and my scouts, to know this business and to know players. Wouldn't you think these people who complained about the trades would have at least waited until they saw who the hell we got?"

What the North Stars had obtained, through trades, after four years of business, were Gump Worsley, Barry Gibbs, Tom Reid, Ted Harris, Jean-Paul Parise, Ted Hampson, Bob Nevin, Danny Grant, Jude Drouin, Doug Mohns, Dennis Hextall, Murray Oliver, Terry Caffery, Charlie Burns and Gordon Labossiere — 15 players on their roster as they headed into the 1971-72 season.

One trade, especially, rankled the local scribes, because this deal brought Doug Mohns to the Stars for Danny O'Shea. O'Shea, who had been signed in June of 1968 after playing with the Canadian Olympic team, was a big, fast, handsome center who had become highly popular with the Minnesota following.

A newspaper man confronted The Bird after the trade.

"That's the worst deal you've ever made, and I'm going to write it that way," said the writer.

That criticism stung Blair. He had a high regard for the writer and considered him a close friend among the media men he knew. But while the writer had his job to do, so did The Bird.

"You write whatever you want," said Blair, "but I'm going to tell you something. If it was a bad deal, it's the first bad one I've made, not the worst one. Secondly, you don't know Doug Mohns from a hole in the ground, you just know who Danny O'Shea is."

"I still think it's a bad deal, and I'm going to say so."

"You can do what you want, but just because of what you say doesn't make you any authority that I'm going to listen to. Because if you're right, Walter Bush better hire you and I'll go write your column."

The frank exchange did not alter their friendship, and later the writer told Blair, "You were right on that one, that Mohns is terrific."

Criticism notwithstanding, The Bird never lost sight of his original goal to trade away most of those original draft choices, and he would not make any apologies for his dedication to this cause.

"We were locked into their rules," Blair said, reflecting on the draft. "It was like playing poker and they took all the aces, kings, queens, jacks, tens and nines out of the deck. Now they got all those cards over there and they say, 'Let's play.'

"So, okay, we made all kinds of deals. But when you make deals, you don't know you're going to be right in every one. I know Jack Adams told me years ago — and he built more hockey clubs in Detroit than you can shake a stick at and traded more hockey players than any guy in history — he said 'Don't ever be afraid to make a deal. I've made more bad trades and bad deals than any guy in the history of hockey, but I've made more good ones too, because I've made more trades.' He also told me that if they go bad, I shouldn't look back, because if you start looking back you are going to get scared."

Within four years, only two of the initial draft choices were still with the North Stars: Cesare Maniago, whose spectacular play in the nets had saved the Stars from many embarrassing nights, and that explosive young man on right wing who had become known to everyone around simply as Goldy.

Blair absorbed almost as much criticism for not dealing away the erratic right winger as he did for trading those who went. If he was bull-headed over the matter, it was due to his unshakable faith that under the surface storm that seemed to hurl the blonde youngster into one controversy after another was the potential of a great hockey player. Then, too, The Bird had some understanding of what it was like to be blessed with a quick and violent temper. The two seemed to have been spewed out of the same tempest.

That first year in Minnesota would not soon be forgotten by those close to the North Stars. There was pathos, humor, excitement . . . tragedy.

Masterton's death following an injury in a mid-season game was the first death in the 54-year history of the National Hockey League. They have an award now, in his name, which goes to the North Star player voted by his teammates as most valuable to the team during the season.

The North Stars were not a good hockey team that first year. That they came within one game of making the finals of the Stanley Cup playoffs was due only to the driving, demanding, imploring urgings of

Wren Blair. The Bird had devoted the better part of a lifetime to hockey. When he was five years old he could rattle off every roster of every team in the National Hockey League, and this talent his parents used to entertain guests. In those early years, like many Canadian boys, he played hockey from morning until night. He was out on a pond all day during the winter, and when he came home at night he played in the driveway under a street lamp. After supper he and his brother would each take a table spoon and sit at opposite ends of the kitchen, batting a tennis ball between them. The door frames served as the outer edges of the goal. Sometimes the flying tennis ball would hit their mother in the head. Hockey is a tough game for mothers.

"At home," said Blair, who was born in Lindsay, Ontario, "you could hardly get up and down the streets because of the hockey games going on. In the summer we used to rent the rink and put on roller skates and play hockey, but that was a little bit much."

The Bird played hockey through Junior B, but then went into the army. The system is so precise and so exacting that there is no way to make up for such lost time. When he returned from the army, Blair was too old for Junior A hockey, but his love of the game led him into the business end of the operation. He became a shrewd businessman and a coach who detested losing. He prowled behind the bench, red of face, his curly dark hair in disarray, bellowing at his players, the officials, anyone and anything that came between him and victory.

That he tore into his players was due to his own personal philosophy of life and the circumstances he faced.

"It's when a guy has talent and is not giving it that I get mad. It's guys like Goldy that are going to get hell, guys that I know have got it and aren't giving it."

In training camp once a young rookie was not living up to the expectations of the North Stars, and Blair had his coach yank the youngster off the ice and sent to his office.

"Look, young man," said Blair, "you better make up your mind about one thing. You're no National Leaguer yet, in my opinion, but you've got a lot of talent and I traded for talent. But I'm not putting up with this kind of nonsense one bit. When my coach blows that whistle out there, you move or else you get your bag packed and get out of here."

A short time later the rookie, who had been bothered by the lack of a contract, reached an agreement with the North Stars. With that problem out of the way, Jude Drouin went on to become runner-up for rookie-of-the-year honors in 1970-71.

Things had a way of happening to The Bird that relieved some of the tension and pressure that first year. In just their third game ever, the Stars were playing in the Long Beach arena and the Los Angeles Kings' Lowell McDonald had gotten around the Stars' Mike McMahon on the boards and scored a goal while Minnesota had a man advantage. The period ended and Blair was steaming. He stormed into the locker room with a trench coat in his hand and fired it at McMahon.

"Damn you, Mike, how many times have I told you . . ."

As he threw the coat his foot slipped on an orange peeling and The Bird went sliding flat on his back, talking all the while. He scrambled to his feet, furious now, and kicked a garbage pail, which flew up into the air, papers in it fluttering down all over the room like a February snowfall in Minnesota. In kicking the pail he injured his foot, and he hopped about, holding the foot in his hand and talking all the while. The players held towels against their faces to restrain the laughter.

The next day, on an airplane to Pittsburgh, a club official who had walked in while Blair was on his back the previous night, said, "Say, can I ask you a question?"

"Sure," said The Bird.

"What kind of a play were you trying to demonstrate when I came in yesterday?"

The incident was not mentioned again until late that season when Blair was walking down a slippery corridor at an airport, and as he passed Cesare Maniago going the other way, The Bird's foot slipped a little.

"Watch the orange peels," said Cesare, smiling.

Blair broke into laughter.

Once during a practice the team members became involved in an argument over free public appearances on behalf of the North Star organization. Blair became so angry over the bickering and so disgusted with the workout that he blew his whistle and ordered the team off the ice. He was furious, and as he skated off the ice he threw a hockey stick into the empty players' bench.

The stick hit on its toe and came sailing back like a boomerang, striking The Bird right across the beak. Blood flew everywhere. One of the players tried to get a hold of him, but he pushed him off. "Get your hands off me!" he growled.

Then he stalked away and down into a private room under the stands.

"The whole rink was spinning, but there's no way I was going to collapse in front of those guys," Blair said later.

On the way out of the arena after that practice The Bird, black and blue around the eyes so that his face resembled that of a raccoon, passed a group of his players.

"See! See what I go through for you guys!" he said.

There were many incidents of a like nature that first year, because the pressure had everyone wound up tight. The Stars needed a playoff spot to establish major league hockey in the Twin Cities, and everyone from top management to the players knew it and was working for it.

So intent was he on winning that first year that Blair drove his players well beyond their natural ability. What he was trying to do was to get every man on that club to play 120 per cent. The extra twenty per cent, multiplied by eighteen players, meant the team would play 360 per cent above its collective ability. That's what it had to have to survive against the East. A lot of those first-year players gave that kind of effort. But it was too much to expect of any human being to play that much over his head for a long period of time. Some of them fell by the wayside the second year.

It had been Blair's intention from the beginning to coach only until he found the right man as bench boss — hopefully after that first season — but circumstances always seemed to be working against him.

In the second season he had turned the coaching duties over to John Muckler, while the Stars were in second place in the West. Muckler, who had had great success in the minor leagues, inherited a team that would go into a long slump. Minnesota plummetted from second place to last place in the standings, and the hockey public was in a state of revolt. Muckler was released from the position, and The Bird came back to the bench. The North Stars made a late season rally, and came within a hair of reaching the playoffs once again.

Blair had tried to hire Jack Gordon, long-time player, coach and general manager of Cleveland in the American Hockey League, but Gordon then had a long-term contract and a strong loyalty to his present organization, and would not leave.

Thus, when the third season started, The Bird was still behind the bench, driving his players and his blood pressure to new heights. His health prevented him from finishing that season as coach. Among his trades was one that brought an old acquaintance to the North Stars. Back in the days when he was building the Whitby Dunlops into a world champion,

The Bird had sought out a young man who had been a promising hockey prospect until suffering a severe skull fracture in 1954. If Charlie Burns, who had been born in Detroit but was raised in the Canadian hockey factories, could play again, Blair wanted him. Burns did play again, on that world amateur championship team.

From then on he was in professional hockey, playing with various minor league teams as well as Detroit, Boston, California and Oakland of the NHL. Once during his nomadic career he had been playing coach of San Francisco. Burns was acquired from the Stars' expansion cousin, Pittsburgh, and upon being reunited with The Bird, told him:

"If there is anything I can ever do to help you, please let me know."

When Blair began to suffer from high blood pressure, he went to Burns and asked him to preside at practice sessions. Later Burns took over the coaching duties. During his tenure behind the bench the Stars had suffered through a non-winning streak that came very close to setting an NHL record. They went for twenty games without a win, and dropped so far back in the standings that their chances of winning a playoff spot that year were remote. Unable to cope with this miserable state of affairs, Burns once again laced up his skates to become a playing coach. The Stars came from a long way back to get into the playoffs.

Charlie didn't look good in a business suit, anyway.

Blair touched the lives of many young men in his

stormy career, and in such a way that few would forget him. If he was a tough guy, that was the result of his own hot-headed youth and the lessons he had learned along the way.

The only teachers he had remembered from school were the ones that had stepped all over him, and this would make an impact upon him later.

"When we won the World Amateur Championship in 1958," said The Bird, "the first people I heard from by wire were those that had been real tough on me in school. They sent me wires saying how proud they were of me. I couldn't believe it, that they felt this way. Then later I began to realize that this is what discipline is all about. The ones that think you've got the most to offer, if they care, they're the ones that are going to be the hardest on you."

This philosophy Blair had taken with him into the ranks of professional hockey, and he practiced it in an unrelenting way. He would not tolerate a young player giving less than 100 per cent, and his determination in this matter sometimes involved a player's wife.

He believed that a wife had a strong influence on a hockey player's career.

"I think a wife that lets her husband come home and cry on her shoulder for getting hell from the coach lets him off the hook and is not going to help him at all. This is human nature, if she is loyal to her husband, but it's not going to help him.

"The public doesn't realize how young these players are. Generally they're just kids away from home for the first time in life and they get in trouble and pop off. No damn kid is going to tell me what to do. I remember things I did at twenty-one or twenty-two that I'd just as soon forget. They're doing the same things, because that's a part of growing up. But I'm not about to let them or their wives change my opinion about something I think they're absolutely out of line about. Very seldom, if you're fair, does a guy ever disagree with that ten years later."

Blair, whose great grandfather had emigrated from Scotland to Canada and had the town of Blair-Hampton named after him, takes great pride in bringing along young players and seeing them develop.

"I think there's a little bit of this protege thing in all of us, or a little bit of a kingmaker," he once said. "Goldy is one of many hockey players I feel that way about. You put a lot of things into their lives. That's what is fun about this game, to see youngsters come along and you rap their knuckles and they're convinced you hate them, but later they come to know differently."

Life is an ongoing cycle of such things. Goldy would not realize for some time that the needle The Bird stuck him with was not intended to cause pain. But he did come to see this, just as The Bird had learned that lesson before him.

"Even though we've had our ups and downs, Wren has really tried to help me," said Goldy. "I've played for some good coaches, but I felt closer to Wren than the others because of the time we were together and the fact he didn't give up on me. When he was coaching he had that ability to get the adrenalin flowing in his players. Sure he was stern, but he was also honest and fair with the players, and they respected him for that. I know he has had a great impact on my career."

Chapter VI

To Chase a Dream

"Look, young man," said The Bird, his irritability showing in his face, "I'm going to make a major league hockey player out of you if it kills both of us. The only thing that bothers me is that I'm not sure I'm going to make it."

Goldy studied Blair's face for a moment, then turned and skated back to where the practice drills were being conducted.

This was Haliburton in the fall of 1967. Few people could spend a month in Haliburton, Ontario, and not be captivated by its immense wilderness beauty. Youngsters by the hundreds, from all over Canada, the United States and even parts of Europe, pay $125 a week to go to a hockey camp there in the summer months. To them it is a time of fun and excitement, and that they receive instructions from some of the best hockey players in the world, with everything else, makes it a fairytale land.

But from the group of young men who went there in the fall of 1967, many would come away bitterly disappointed over their short visit, while the others would remember little of its charm. They just weren't paying attention.

Wren Blair operates the summer camp and hockey school there (called Haliburton Hockey Haven), and when the newly-franchised Minnesota North Stars of the National Hockey League were casting about for a training camp that first year, it was the logical place to go.

Goldy and his bride of less than five months had said their goodbyes after leaving that swank apartment in the basement of the three-story brick house in Niagara, and June had gone to stay with her parents while Goldy headed off to Haliburton.

There he would find a camp that reminded him of his first trip away from home when he had gone to Niagara, because Haliburton was overflowing with hockey players. The North Stars wanted to look at a lot of people before they settled on the eighteen they would take into that first season.

Expansion was a big break for many young hockey players. It offered those who had been only mediocre, and those who didn't have a chance to prove themselves before because of the availability of a lot of other good hockey talent, an opportunity to prove themselves now.

On the trip to Haliburton, Goldy had a lot of time to think, and what he kept saying over and over was probably what every other young player going to that camp said: "Okay, this is it. If you don't make it now, you'll never make it."

Unlike the previous summer, when he had gone to camp with the questionable leg, Goldy went to Haliburton in good physical condition. He had one other edge over most of the young men there. He had played 33 games in the NHL over those two years he was bouncing around between Boston, Oklahoma City and Buffalo. But if this impressed the management, they weren't saying so, because once the two-a-day practice sessions started, their only concern was sorting out the eighteen best hockey players in that camp, and the names and faces were of little consequence.

Blair, who had decided to handle the coaching duties as well as serve as general manager that first year, saw as his immediate task the creation of a team with unity and spirit. The players invited to camp had come off the rosters of many teams, each with its own style of play. In addition, there were some animosities between players who had been on opposite sides in the past, and these had to be smoothed over if unity was to be achieved.

To provide an atmosphere conducive to such purposes, Blair had the team quartered at Chateau Woodlands Lodge, a comfortable and scenic spa on a lake with the hard-to-handle name of Kashagawigamog. There they lived, two men to a cottage, and dined in a mess hall style setting. But their attention to food would have depressed a mess hall cook.

The rigors of the daily routine were such that there was little time or inclination for recreational pursuits or eating. Goldy arose at 7 a.m. each day, had toast and tea for breakfast, then dressed for the bus trip to the arena in Haliburton. No one ate much for breakfast because there were two hours of hard skating in the morning, and this was not compatible with a stomach full of food.

After the morning workout they were bused back to Chateau Woodlands for lunch, which wasn't much more impressive than breakfast because there would be two more hours of skating in the afternoon. Lunch might consist of a small bowl of ice cream with fruit cocktail, toast and tea.

Following the afternoon workout the aspiring major leaguers were put through calisthenics to keep their muscles loose. The North Stars had imported a physical fitness expert to lead the team in its exercises, and it took superhuman efforts to keep up with him.

In the evening, after a supper of high protein foods like steak and roast beef, they had canoe races in which anything was legal, including upsetting the competition's craft. Goldy was usually out in front in these races, as a matter of survival. He couldn't swim. He just put his head down and paddled for all he was worth.

The routine was monotonous and tiring, and those that stayed with the team could be found in bed as early as 8 p.m. many nights.

Sometimes Goldy's body was so sore that at night he soaked in a bathtub of hot water and epsom salts. When he got up in the morning it felt as though he had casts on both legs, and he had difficulty walking.

There was little leisure time activity in that first camp, but it mattered little, because the energy they possessed was directed toward a single goal: making that North Star lineup. Anything that stood in the way of that purpose was either irrelevant or irritating — like another guy who had the same ambition.

There were some spirited exchanges during that camp.

Fisticuffs were a routine thing, because everyone there was trying to grab a job, and if things weren't going well, the tendency was to lash out at somebody.

Tempers were always on the ragged edge when the players who had been assigned to the Stars' Memphis farm club would beat those still on the roster of the big team. The Memphis players wanted to go up and the others didn't want to go down.

Goldy had a good, if not spectacular, training camp, spiced by an occasional confrontation with The Bird. The Stars had too little talent of NHL caliber not to get the most out of those who possessed it.

But while Blair was a source of irritation to him off the ice, he was still having his troubles on the ice. In one exhibition game he had one of his numerous encounters with an official, which cost him more money in fines than he and June had been able to save all that previous summer.

Once during that training camp the Stars had played an exhibition game in Hamilton, and June had travelled the forty miles from Niagara Falls to be with him briefly. They walked the streets of Hamilton for two hours, holding hands like newlyweds of only five months, and then he was gone again.

When the Stars broke camp to go south, Goldy was one of twenty-eight players they took with them. Cesare Maniago, the lanky netminder, was another, and only these two would survive the trades Blair would make in the next four years. Much had been expected of Cesare. The assessment of Goldy was little changed from what it had been when he was running amok in the Bruin chain: if he could control his temper, and if he ever decided he really wanted to be a major leaguer, there were probably few limitations on what he might accomplish.

But meanwhile, Minnesota had some other guys who looked like better immediate prospects, and these were the ones they touted as they headed south. They had taken left winger Dave Balon out of the Montreal organization as their first draft choice; center Ray Cullen was picked second, from the Detroit roster; Bob Woytowich, a Boston defenseman, had been selected third.

Right wing, where Goldy had played ever since he was a small boy, was perhaps the Stars' strongest position. There they had Wayne Connelly, whose bullet shots would get him 35 goals in that first season; Billy Collins, a steady performer drafted from the New York Rangers, and Andre Pronovost, who had scored 67 points for Memphis the previous year. And Goldy.

From Haliburton the Stars went by bus to Toronto, then flew to the Twin Cities. Goldy did not fly with the team. He drove to Niagara to pick up June and the few possessions they had accumulated in their short married life. Everything they owned they were able to pack in the trunk and back seat of the car. They had no furniture to worry about. The car was so tail heavy that the front looked like it was always going uphill. Goldy had to set on a pillow to see out over the hood.

Goldy had never been to Minnesota before, and at one time during the long trip west he told June, "I think we're coming to the ocean pretty soon."

They stayed in a motel that first week in the Twin Cities, with Goldy splitting his time between practice sessions and apartment hunting. Finally they settled in a one bedroom furnished apartment near Met Sports Center that cost them $185 per month. It was a chaotic time for the young couple, and even while they were trying to put down some roots, there was that nagging possibility they, like others in that strange business, always had to consider: tomorrow he could be traded.

The Stars opened their first NHL season at St. Louis, with Bill Masterton scoring their first goal. The game ended in a 2-2 tie. It was a routine start to a perplexing and emotion-filled season. Masterton, whose name shall forever remain in the North Stars' record book for that first goal of that first game, may someday hold another Minnesota record: if Maniago and Goldsworthy are ever traded, he would be the only original North Star never dealt away.

After a trip to the West Coast, the North Stars went to Bloomington for their home opener, against California. A crowd of 12,951 was there for the occasion, and the Stars did not disappoint them, skating to a 3-1 win — their first victory in the NHL.

Minnesota struck early in the second period. Mini-center Andre Boudrias, who had been purchased from Montreal, picked up a loose puck just inside his own blue line and fed it up ice to first draft-choice Dave Balon. Balon raced into the California zone with a muscular blonde kid streaking in on his left. There was but one Seal defender back, and he made a move against Balon, who hit Goldy with a perfect pass. Goldy chipped the puck past goalie Charlie Hodge. So Goldy went into the North Stars' record book too, having scored their first goal ever at Met Sports Center.

Goldy would not repeat the performance with great frequency that first year. He spent a lot of time going in and out of the penalty box and counting out fine money. One young fan wrote him during that first year: "Dear Mr. Goldsworthy: I'm starting a fan club for you because I like the way you fight. I wish you would send me twenty autographed pictures of you."

Clarence Campbell and Wren Blair were not starting any fan clubs for Goldy, and the only autographs they came after were on the bottom of the checks he would deliver for his spurious conduct on the ice.

In a game against Toronto, J.P. Parise, Goldy and Andre Boudrias got a three-on-one break, with Goldsworthy carrying the puck in on goalie Bruce Gamble. The second guessers said Goldy should have shot, but he didn't. Instead he passed to Parise, who slammed one far wide of the net. When the period ended, Blair stormed up to Goldy and said, "That'll be a $25 fine! When you can see the whites of their eyes, you're supposed to fire!"

Campbell relieved Goldy of something approaching $500 that first season — either through fines or loss of salary during suspensions.

In a game against the Philadelphia Flyers, Goldy had knocked down linesman John D'Amico, and this bit of mayhem got him a three-day suspension without pay and a $150 fine. Campbell said the penalty was severe because of the similar incident involving the right winger in that exhibition game, when he was separated from $200 in fine money.

"I'm sick over losing all that money," said Goldy, when the fine and suspension were announced. "This is a pretty stiff penalty. Sure, I was wrong, but consider the situation. Here we are, getting beat 4-2 at home, and that brassy little Forbes Kennedy is running around belting one guy and mouthing off to another. It reached the point where I couldn't stand him anymore. When he charged into one of our guys on the boards, I started to go after him. D'Amico got in the way."

There were times during that first season when the Stars' frustrations against the established Eastern teams were more humorous than pathetic.

When Minnesota went into Detroit to play the Red Wings, Goldy was on a line playing against that famous trio of Gordy Howe, Frank Mahovlich and Alex Delvecchio. The Stars skated furiously after the puck, but if the three weren't in a scoring mood they just held onto the puck, passing it back and forth between them while the Stars' frustrations mounted.

When he skated to the bench after a line change, Goldy said, "They should throw in another puck and let us play, too."

In a later meeting with the Red Wings, when the Stars were badly in need of a win to stay close in the race for a playoff spot, Minnesota sent J.P. Parise out in an attempt to check the Howe line. In a very short time the Stars were down, 4-0.

"Just think if I hadn't checked them," said Parise when he came off the ice.

Much to the surprise of hockey watchers, the expansion teams did win some of those games with the East that first year. Not many, but some. It would have been total disaster for the West if all of the established teams had come at them as the New York Rangers did. The Rangers lost only two games to the expansion teams all season.

By mid-season of that first year the Stars had already undergone a partial face-lifting through trades. They had picked up Parise and Milan Marcetta in that five-for-two trade with Toronto, among others.

Parise would remember his first week in the Twin Cities because of the unexpected kindnesses offered him and Marcetta by the Stars third line center, Bill Masterton. The two new North Stars had been put up in a motel when they arrived, and that first day of practice Masterton had gone out of his way to come by the motel and take them to the rink, even though they had never been acquainted before.

"I didn't get much of a chance to know him well," Parise said later, "but he was just one of those nice guys you run into sometime. One night several families got together for a birthday party, kids and all, and the adults were in one room talking while the kids were playing in another room. Bill was sitting in the middle of the floor playing with all those kids. He just loved them."

Masterton centered a line with Goldy on right wing and Teddy Taylor, a sixth-round draft pick from

Detroit, on the left, until the popular center was injured in January, 1968. He died January 15.

While Goldy's temper got him into a lot of scrapes that season, Blair's explosions often influenced the course of events for the entire team. In a game against Philadelphia, with his team trailing 2-1, The Bird needled a linesman for indecisiveness in making an icing call. The linesman told the referee, who assessed a penalty against the Minnesota bench.

Blair then exploded in the general direction of the referee. A second penalty was called, this one for delay of the game.

Now two men short, the Stars managed to skate out the penalties without further damage, and generated some momentum as a result. They got the tying goal.

"We needed something to get us going," said Blair, "and skating out those penalties was the perfect lift. It turned the game around."

The Stars went into the final two games of the season, both against St. Louis, hanging on to third place by a thin margin. In the first of these two games Minnesota had a 2-1 lead with only a few minutes to play when the Stars were assessed a penalty. St. Louis scored the tying goal and later another, to win, 3-2.

When the two teams went to the Twin Cities for the final contest, the Blues won again, 5-3, dropping the Stars into fourth place. St. Louis pocketed the

$750 per man for a third place finish, and the Stars settled for fourth place money of $250 each.

For the Stanley Cup playoffs Minnesota drew the Los Angeles Kings in the first round. The teams battled to a 3-3 deadlock in games, each winning all the games on its home ice. The Stars narrowly avoided elimination in the sixth contest, trailing 3-1 after two periods. Goldy led a third period rally that tied the score at 3-3, getting one goal. Then, in the first overtime game ever played at Met Sports Center, the blonde winger fought off a check and got the puck to Milan Marcetta, who stroked in the winning goal.

The teams went back to the Los Angeles Forum for the seventh and final game, with the Kings favored to win. But the Stars exploded for a club record five goals in the second period, and buried Los Angeles 9-4, to advance to the Cup semi-finals series against St. Louis, which had ousted Philadelphia. Goldy, skating harder than he had all season, scored two goals in that deciding game.

When they moved on to play St. Louis, the Stars lost the crucial home ice advantage for one game, because of a scheduling conflict. The operators of Met Sports Center apparently had not consulted the same fortune teller as Wren Blair, because they had booked the Ice Follies into the Met right during the playoffs.

The bruising series went the full seven games nonetheless, five of them at St. Louis, and four going into sudden death overtime. Goldy, as he had done against Los Angeles, ignited the Stars' attack throughout the Blues' series, and his performance brought back memories to a university hockey coach, of the first time he had seen Goldy.

"The Canadian Amateur Hockey Association was staging a clinic for coaches in Kingston, Ontario in the summer of 1964," the coach said. "Goldy had played with the Niagara Falls Junior A team that year and was on hand to demonstrate the fundamentals we were trying to teach. He was about eighteen then and you could see at the time that he had the potential to play in the NHL. He was built like Gordy Howe, with sloping, powerful shoulders. He had tremendous natural equipment, was very strong and was a hard-nosed kid who wouldn't take anything. You knew then that if Goldy did make it, he not only would be a superior hockey player but a very colorful one. This guy is going to be a great gate attraction."

Goldy finished the playoffs that first year with eight goals and seven assists, one of those goals against St. Louis coming after a typical verbal attack from The Bird. The winger had given the Stars a 1-0 lead with a first period score in the sixth game of the series, but St. Louis had scored to tie it up in the second while Goldy's line was on the ice.

"We're even," said Blair, when Goldy skated off. "Your job was to clear that rebound from in front of Cesare. You better get the hell out there and score another to make up for that one!"

Goldy scored again on his next line shift and the Stars went on to a 5-1 win.

In an interview after that game the Stars' right winger was asked what had accounted for his scoring spree in the playoffs.

"I think it was that three-game suspension they tossed at me toward the end of the season. I did a lot of thinking those four or five days that I wasn't able to play. I told myself that I'd been taking a lot of unnecessary penalties. You know the kind, where some guy raps me and I either go after him right away or wait until I get the chance to take a run at him. I decided I was going to turn over a new leaf and make a strong finish."

The Stars ultimately lost the series in the second sudden death overtime of the seventh game. And, though he did not play in the finals, Goldy's fifteen points led all scoring in the Cup playoffs.

His performance so pleased Wren Blair that The Bird gave back all the fine money he had assessed Goldy back in training camp at the beginning of the season. Some observers had said when that camp was over that Goldy owed Blair more in fines than Blair owed him in salary.

"I guess I'm the only guy who ever paid to go through training camp," said Goldy, at the end of the season. "Wren was pretty good about it though, and he gave it all back after the playoffs. There was no interest though. It was more like a savings program."

The inconsistent winger, in spite of possessing a shot that had been clocked at slightly more than 100 miles per hour, had finished the regular season with just 14 goals, 22 assists and 68 minutes in the penalty box. His accomplishments were not notable, unless the fines were considered an achievement. Because of his erratic play and his short fuse, Goldy had attracted a lot of attention among the North Stars' following, and it was not always favorable. He was colorful, and he generated an aura of excitement when he wheeled with the puck at center ice in those long, powerful strides, knees bent, and came charging across the opposition's blue line in a reckless way, rarely trying to finesse the defense with fancy maneuvers but instead going right over a man, and the consequences be damned.

But excitement was not necessarily compatible with effectiveness, and this latter many of the Minnesota faithfuls questioned. They felt Goldy was hurting the team with unnecessary penalties. Blair had taken severe criticism for not unloading the winger in a trade, and it was not until that first Stanley Cup playoff that his refusal to do so would be vindicated.

"That was some of the best hockey I ever saw Goldy play," said The Bird. "He was skating like crazy and checking well and scoring. Those were tremendous pressure games, and he seemed to thrive on it.

"Still, he had annoyed and depressed me during the regular season with bonehead plays. I would tell him he was going down to Memphis, but in my heart I knew Goldy was too good a prospect not to keep with us. I chewed him out all year.

"One thing I always did though . . . whenever he played good I told him that after the game. I'm a great believer in the theory that the same hand that does the spanking is the one that better pat you on the back.

"I know Goldy, and if I go by him and say, 'You played a hell of a game tonight!' he'd just glow. Everybody needs a pat on the back. I think it all paid off, because in the playoffs he grew from a boy into an adult."

When that tragic, chaotic, unpredictable season of 1967-68 finally ended, The Bird had no apologies to make, either for his team or his faith in Goldy.

"This guy knows how to play the game," he said, "if he can get himself to forget being an arbitrator. I've always said his potential is unlimited and now I think some doubting Thomases see what I mean."

Chapter VII

Cy's Diner Isn't the Ritz

Christmas in Minnesota is beautiful, unless you are looking at it from Memphis, Tennessee. There is a lot of country in between to obstruct the view. To the top scorer of the Stanley Cup playoffs in the spring of 1968, traveling the streets of Memphis during the holiday season later that year was a lonely, bitter experience.

The rest of the country may have been in a festive mood, but Goldy was disturbed and depressed. His wife, June, was back in Minneapolis with Tammy Lynn, that little blue-eyed blonde who was less than three months old, and here Goldy was in Memphis with Christmas coming on and he hadn't done any of his shopping. Anyway, Goldy was not in a shopping mood. All he wanted was a plane ticket to the Twin Cities.

For Goldy, the 1968-69 NHL season held the promise of great things. He had showed his detractors a few things in those playoff games the previous season, and there was every reason to think he would pick up right where he left off. Goldy had spent the better part of the summer thinking that, and he was not in particularly good condition when the second training camp started.

Camp was again held at Haliburton, but this time the players were quartered at Blair's facilities about eight miles back in the woods on Lake Koshlong. There they lived in cabins of ten to fifteen men each. The setting was familiar to Goldy, since he had spent most of the summer after that first season working as an instructor in Blair's hockey school. June had gone with him to Haliburton for the summer, and they had lived in a large cabin there. But when the Stars went into training in September, she had gone to Kitchener to stay with Bill's mother and await the arrival of their first child.

This event transpired on September 18, 1968, and Goldy had some kind of premonition about the occurrence. He had telephoned June at supper time that day.

"What's going on?" he asked.

"Nothing yet," said June.

"I had a feeling that something might be happening."

"No, I'm fine."

Later that evening June went to the hospital and gave birth to Tammy Lynn, like her father a blue-eyed blonde. But she was prettier than Goldy.

In the recovery room June telephoned the camp in Haliburton. Goldy had to be called from the ice. She was crying when he answered. "I'm sorry I didn't have a boy."

Blair gave Goldy the next day off, and he drove to Kitchener to meet his new dependent. Then he was gone again, to make an exhibition game.

June had a better autumn than Goldy.

Even though he had worked at the hockey camp, where his popularity with the youngsters was unmatched by other instructors there, he had not paid attention to his conditioning as he did the previous year. Consequently he got off to a sluggish start, and this would lead to a series of depressing events later.

Coming off that impressive playoff series, Goldy figured that all he had to do was lace up his skates and everything would fall in place that second season. This overconfidence rapidly vanished as his difficulties on the ice mounted, and not only did he begin to lose confidence in himself, but also the management was becoming alarmed.

When the Stars went south for the start of their second season, they had little of the spirit and drive they had mustered for the Cup playoffs, and Goldy became the chief source of irritation to Blair.

They did open with a 5-1 win over Oakland, with Goldy driving in the first score. But the points became as rare as whooping cranes thereafter, even though Goldy was trying to forge a new image.

"I'm trying to stay away from penalties," he said early in the season. "I just wish the goals came as easily as penalties. I don't want to be identified as a policeman. I just like to score."

He would not deliver on his good intentions.

Blair had handed the Stars' coaching duties to John Muckler, and Minnesota had taken a nose-dive shortly thereafter.

Muckler was particularly displeased with the play of Goldy, Mike McMahon and Andre Boudrias when the Stars took a 4-0 whipping at Boston, and he told Blair so.

"I want those three sent to the minors immediately," Muckler said.

"There's no way I'm going to have guys playing in the minors on major league money," Blair said. "There's a clause in their contracts that says if they don't perform properly that they can be suspended indefinitely for indifferent play. If you want me to invoke that clause, I will. But I'm not sending them to the minors."

"Fine, I want that clause invoked," said Muckler.

The suspensions were announced.

Shortly thereafter the North Star players held a meeting, and the consensus was that if the team was going bad, all of them were at least partly at fault. They did not feel the three being singled out should be blamed for the team's difficulties, so they went to Blair and stated their case, asking that the suspensions be lifted. Blair honored the request, then issued a statement:

"I gave all three of those guys raises varying from 30 to 50 per cent. Maybe I was too generous. But I'm not going to merely send them down to the minor leagues and let them collect major league money. This team simply has to start producing on the ice, and I hope the meeting we had will shake them out of whatever has ailed them."

It didn't. Minnesota went into December playing like Santa Claus, giving away games with cheery abandon, and this precedent would plague them in the following Decembers. With one third of the

season gone, Goldy had only three goals and one
assist, and some people besides the frustrated winger
were plenty unhappy over this meager output. Like
The Bird. Throughout the first season Blair had
resisted many an impulse to send Goldy to the
minors, and that time he had been right. But now the
entire team was adrift in a sea of mediocrity, and it
was time to rock the boat.

"Goldy," said Blair, when the star of the 1968 Cup
playoffs had settled into a chair in The Bird's office at
Met Sports Center, "I think you should go down to
Memphis for awhile to get yourself mentally
prepared. It's not that we don't need you here, we do
need you, and this is why I'm doing it. Maybe it will
make you realize what you have here and you'll
appreciate it much more."

In spite of that depressing decision, Goldy would
fare far better than the other two players in trouble.
Within two weeks, Boudrias and McMahon would be
traded to the Chicago Black Hawks in a move that
brought capable young defenseman Tom Reid to the
North Stars.

Muckler issued a brief statement: "Goldsworthy
is still young and the reason he was farmed out instead of traded or sold is that we still believe he'll
turn into a good hockey player." Muckler would be
gone when his forecast proved accurate a year later.

The Bird did not take his own action lightly. He
had believed in Goldy, had suffered through all that
criticism the year before for not putting him on the
trading block, and was personally fond of the handsome blonde young man with the temperament much
like his own.

Later he would say: "There's nothing easy about sending a guy to the minors. But you say to yourself, 'Suppose I don't do this now, maybe he will go to the minors permanently in another few years.' How much good have you done his career then?"

After delivering the bitter news to Goldy, Blair telephoned June.

"I don't want you to get all shook up over this, but I'm sending Bill down to Memphis. I'm only going to leave him there two weeks, but don't you tell him that. We'll get him home for Christmas. I'm worried about him and I've got to shake him up, but if you tell him when he's coming back, that will undo what we're trying to do."

"Don't worry. I'm as mad at him as you are," said June.

"Do you people like that major league money, or would you like to get along on that minor league money again?"

"Are you kidding!"

"Well then, you better get after that big dumb husband of yours."

Goldy's reaction to the demotion was predictable. He was deeply depressed and he thought of quitting. But he was trapped in the consequences of his own dreams. There was nothing he could quit for, having devoted his formative years to hockey to the exclusion of any other formal training.

"I thought I would pack it in," he said later. "That's the first thing you always say when the going gets tough. But then you think it over and talk with your family and the management, and you decide it's not as if they've put a gun to your head. They're trying to do the best for you, really. It's when they stop looking after you or stop trying to help you that you're in trouble, and you may as well say goodbye because you're all done. Once I realized this, I went down to Memphis."

Goldy had been to Memphis before, on short visits when he was still in the Boston chain and playing with Oklahoma City, but minor league cities don't look the same once you've been to the big show.

The differences were dramatic. Instead of dining at the Ritz, they were eating at Cy's Diner, because the meal allowances were marginal. The minor league teams flew by DC3, rather than the big jets, and the players always scanned the sky nervously before taking off in one of those prop jobs. Unlike the jets, the DC3 would fly right through, not over, the thunderheads.

Goldy lived in a hotel room in Memphis, and he was a lonely, brooding young man. His only contact with his family was an occasional telephone call to June. He did not want to tell his troubles to his parents, but they followed his progress through calls to June. They sent word through her that they knew he would come back, and this tireless confidence on their part was something Goldy always remembered in a sentimental way. Later, when he did come back and was invited to speak at father-and-son banquets, he would tell the audience that he was where he was because of his parents' faith in him.

"You have to have somebody behind you to pat

you on the back and tell you it's tough but to hang in there and keep trying," he would explain.

If Goldy was sentimental and dejected that Christmas season, he did not allow his brooding introspection to leave the hotel room with him when he went out to play a game. He was angry, and, because of this, was devastating on right wing for Memphis.

He was mad at himself for not putting forth the effort he knew he should have when he was on top, and he was determined to show the management and the people back in the Twin Cities that he was no fly-by-night hockey player who could be sent down and not fight back.

Memphis played one game at Fort Worth, a Detroit Red Wing farm team, during Goldy's two weeks there, and going into the rink he crossed paths with Peter Mahovlich, the giant younger brother of the great Frank Mahovlich.

"What the heck are you doing here?" asked Goldy.

"Don't ask. What are you doing here?" said Mahovlich.

The next time they saw each other Mahovlich was in a Red Wing uniform and Goldy in North Star duds, and when they passed on the ice Goldy said: "You look a lot bigger than in Fort Worth. Everything looks a lot bigger than in Fort Worth."

If Memphis used the "home" and "road" hockey player system, as Oklahoma City had when Goldy was first in the minors, the system did not apply to him. He played in six games, both at home and on the road, and scored five goals and six assists.

He was mentally prepared for the trip back.

"Goldy, they're calling you back," said Memphis coach Milan Marcetta, who had played with the North Stars only a year before.

"I've been waiting for the call. Those greasy hot dogs aren't agreeing with me."

It was Christmas Eve when he flew into the Twin Cities. He still hadn't bought any presents, so after the reunion with June and the infant Tammy, he started out the apartment door to beat the closing of the stores.

"Please take out the garbage," said June.

"Fine," said Goldy.

Goldy got into the elevator, still holding the garbage, and pushed the button for the first floor. Between the second and first floors the elevator became stuck.

There was no telephone in the elevator, but rather a button that allegedly summoned help in case of such an emergency. Goldy pushed the button. Nothing happened. He pushed it again and again, and hollered for help for almost an hour, and all the while it was getting hotter in there and the garbage was stinking up the place.

Right then he said to himself, "This is absolutely the worst that can happen to me. Things have to start going my way after this."

They did. Not only was he freed from that oppressive cage in time to beat the closing of the stores, but also the puck started to do things for him that it hadn't before he was farmed out. In his first game back his unabated fury lifted the Stars to a 4-4 tie with Los Angeles. Then came the Chicago Black Hawks, and though the Stars absorbed a 5-2 beating, Goldy was praised for his aggressive play. But along with those happenings went the usual. Goldy was assessed game misconduct penalties in both contests.

Still, Coach Muckler, who became general manager of the Cleveland Barons, was impressed with his play, and said after the Black Hawk game:

"I think Goldy was our best player out there. He lifted the team with his hustle. He did the same thing in L.A. He wouldn't hit anybody earlier."

This last statement did not seem to square with the records, since Goldy was well on the way toward setting a team record for penalty minutes when he was shipped off to Memphis.

In his third game back, this one against the Bruins, whose farm system he had cut his teeth in (those that he wasn't losing), Goldy put forth his finest effort of the season in a 2-2 tie.

While he continued to be abrasive, he was also aggressive, so much so that when Wren Blair again took over the coaching duties in late season, in an attempt to rally the Stars, he praised his winger for his inspired play.

"Goldy didn't complain when we shipped him to Memphis," said The Bird. "He went down with the idea of returning soon. Now he is playing as good hockey as anybody on our team. He's a real battler."

When the Stars went into Pittsburgh for a crucial

game, Goldy was back in the doghouse for committing a couple of errors, and Blair's anger kindled the fires in his right winger. Goldy charged up the Stars and led them to a 3-1 win.

"I guess he plays best when he gets mad at me," sighed Blair, when the game was over. "But he assured us of the two points and those might turn out to be big ones for us."

The Pittsburgh game was a memorable one in Goldy's career, because it was there that he did a little dance that later would capture the fancy of North Star partisans.

Goldy was so happy when he scored the go-ahead goal that he brought his right leg up in the air, cocked his knee, then thrust the leg forward. As he glided toward center ice on his left skate, he pumped his right fist in piston-like fashion.

The Goldy Shuffle was born.

Later, the origination of the shuffle would become one of the first questions strangers asked him, and he would say in jest: "I hit a paper clip and lost my balance."

Goldy did not jest much after being called back up from Memphis. He was wound up like a rubber band on a 10-cent airplane, and was flying the same way: unpredictably, in great bursts of energy, at times crashing violently.

If he was upset when he went to the locker room after a period, he might hurl his stick against the wall. Nobody slept in the locker room when Goldy was there.

His teammates put a sign on the bench where he dressed.

It simply said: "EXPLOSIVES", in big black letters.

Goldy finished that season with 14 goals, matching his first year's output. Eleven of them came after being called up. He was far from being among the team leaders in scoring, but he was not used on the power play in those days. This alone — the power play opportunity — is generally conceded to add up to fifteen goals per season for hard-shooting forwards.

Goldy's performance was solid, if not spectacular, but it was not enough to lift the sagging North Stars, who finished in a tie for fifth place and out of the Stanley Cup playoffs.

Despite his two weeks' absence from the lineup, Goldy did manage to set a club record that season. He accumulated 108 minutes in penalties.

Although they did not make the playoffs, the Stars had made some trades that were aimed at building a solid foundation for the future. The key acquisition was that of Danny Grant, a rookie left winger obtained in a trade with the Montreal Canadiens. Grant won the NHL Rookie-of-the-Year honors on the strength of 34 goals and 31 assists in that 1968-69 season. The Stars also picked up Tom Reid, a big defenseman acquired in a trade with Chicago, and Lou Nanne, who had played for the U.S. Olympic team and could operate at either forward or defense.

The season had not been a total disaster for Goldy and, in fact, may have been the turning point in his stormy but brief career. When it was over, there was no bitterness over the things that happened, but rather an honest appraisal of where he had been and why.

"I think it's good for a hockey player to experience the minors," he said when the season ended. "But I hope I never see Memphis again. When I went down, maybe I hadn't experienced the minors enough. I don't think I had a full bite of the NHL and didn't fully realize how great it is to be here and to play here against the top competition.

"These days, with the expansion, there are a lot of young players coming right out of Junior A hockey into the NHL, which is great for them. But they don't know what the minors are like, which makes it harder to appreciate the big league. When I was at Buffalo we would be on a bus like ten or twelve hours over a weekend, and eating at greasy hamburger places. I think that was good, because I look around now at what I have, and I appreciate it a lot more."

Chapter VIII

It's Tough to Score
from the Penalty Box

Out among the woods and lakes and streams of Ontario there is a pretty little golf course that meanders over some steep hills. It is a quiet place, and in the solitude of the morning with the sun caressing the dew on the grass, it is a proper setting for contemplation.

Every day during the summer of 1969 a young man went alone to that picturesque retreat to do battle with his resisting body and something not quite so definable that rested within him, always ready to explode in a fit of temper. He had been undisciplined and, at times, uncontrollable, throughout most of the life he reflected upon as he traveled the hills and valleys of that golf course. If he had not possessed some fine natural abilities, people might have given up on him a long time ago and then, perhaps, he would have fallen by the wayside and become a Falcon for the rest of his life.

Goldy grew a lot — physically and emotionally — on that hilly little golf course near Haliburton, even if those who might have seen him there thought he was a madman. He found some old tire chains, and he wrapped thirty pounds of these around his shoulders each day, then started to run. He ran from the first tee to the first green, did five pushups, ran from the second tee to the second green, and did more pushups. This body-torturing routine covered three miles every day, and in the monotony there was much time to wrestle with that inner thing that had always stood between what he had been and what hockey people said he could be.

"You could be as good as Bobby Hull . . ."

"He reminded me of Gordy Howe . . ."

The comparisons had not always been the same, but the models weren't bad.

Once before, in the Stanley Cup playoffs at the end of that first season, Goldy had promised June that he was going to try to curb his irritability, and if his accomplishments in the playoffs were the measure, he had been successful that time. But it had not lasted, and during that tumultuous second season, after he had again set his sights on staying out of trouble, he had logged his club-record 108 minutes in penalties.

There were times when it appeared that Goldy was trying to homestead the penalty box.

Goldy learned something about discipline that summer on the golf course. He drove his body as he had never done before, and if he could stand up to this kind of punishing physical discipline, there must be something that could be done about that temper.

Still, some measure of retaliation was essential to survival in the big league. Some pretty fair hockey players have been literally muscled out of the National Hockey League by what has become a sort of cave-man ritual. This time-honored practice is not a challenge to a man's playing ability — it is assumed he would not be there if he didn't have it. Rather it is a methodical test of his courage and toughness. A young man taking to the ice in his first NHL game can expect to be the object of some rugged body checking by hardened professionals who are experts at such things. If he does not retaliate, the tough guys will keep coming at him until his effectiveness is diminished by the pounding he has taken. No other team sport has a comparable ritual.

This custom has some tell-tale side effects: it can quickly determine if a young player will over-react, thus picking up what are referred to as "cheap" penalties, and giving the opposition the crucial one-man advantage on the ice.

Goldy's greatest handicap all along had been his inclination for instant retaliation. He did not look kindly upon those bruising checks, and any such attack upon him he took personally and with a great deal of impatience. The offender would have to pay for his transgression, now, not later.

This was one of the things he thought about as he ran that golf course, wrapped in tire chains. But he also had long talks with Wren Blair at The Bird's hockey school where Goldy was again serving as an instructor before that third season.

Blair reflected on those critical days:

"In our talks we both agreed that Bill's big problem was consistency. He'd look like a million bucks on one shift and then do practically nothing on the next. He had everything a great hockey player needed — an ability to skate, a shot, good hockey sense. He just had to stay out of trouble.

"Off the içe Goldy was always very personable and the kids, especially, just loved him. But when the puck was dropped he was like Jekyl and Hyde. When the pressure of the game got going, he was just way up high."

Goldy's own memories of those early days in the NHL were consistent with the Bird's:

"I think possibly the first couple of years with Minnesota I was a little bit too rambunctuous out there. Maybe I retaliated too much, to prove that they couldn't run me out of the league. I wanted to keep my job and stay in the NHL, and consequently I had a lot of penalty minutes. They were afraid to play me the first couple of seasons because I'd go out there and get a penalty and I'd be hurting the club. A lot of teams in this league were eager for a guy like me to come along because they knew they had a good chance of getting that man advantage.

"I wasn't doing it intentionally to hurt the team; I was just that type of hockey player. When I'd go into the corner to take the puck out, there would be a lot of elbows flying and I'd knock somebody down whether it was wrong or not. You learn that there are certain ways to go into the corner and check without taking a penalty.

"Sometimes when I was a little bit lazy in coming back I might get caught out of position and that's when you get those hooking and tripping penalties by trying to catch up with the play. A lot of penalties are like that — you are trying to make up for a mistake."

Goldy had blamed part of his miseries the preceding year on the fact that he had gone to training camp in poor condition and had gotten off to a bad start. Thereafter, it had been downhill all the way to Memphis. He was determined that this would not happen again.

A lot of players — as many as 80 per cent — looked at training camp as a place to get into condition, and thus went there out of shape. Goldy wanted to be among the twenty per cent arriving in playing condition, there being important advantages to this. For one thing, the coaching staff would quickly see who was in the best shape, and those who were would get a lot of ice time right from the start. This, in turn, had a chain reaction effect. Those who played the most had an opportunity to score more, and if they were scoring, their chances were good for being put on the ice for the power play, which in turn led to even greater scoring opportunities.

The overall result of this, if the theory worked, was that the guys who were scoring in camp would play a lot at the beginning of the season.

When the Stars opened their third training camp, June and the infant Tammy, who had stayed with Goldy that summer while he was instructing at the Haliburton Hockey Haven Boys Camp and running the golf course in chains, returned to the Twin Cities where they had moved into a larger apartment.

There were a lot of new faces in that third camp. The Bird, as always, had been actively seeking talent throughout the spring and summer of 1969. The Stars brought in veteran center Charlie Burns from Pittsburgh, who played hockey with that metal plate in his head and who would become coach of the Stars part of that season; defenseman Barry Gibbs, a hard-nosed youngster obtained in a trade with Boston; and winger Tommy Williams, a Duluth, Minnesota, native and one of the rare Americans to crack the Canadian domination of the NHL, obtained in a trade with Boston.

Goldy was a lean and compact 190 pounds at the start of camp, seventeen pounds less than the year before when he had a dismal start. While 80% of the players were skating to get into shape, he was flying down the right side with so much energy and confidence that even The Bird was impressed.

"This could be the year for Goldy," said Blair, as he watched the big winger's furious pace from the sidelines. "His attitude is much, much better than last year at this time. His biggest problem is that he has had more bad games than good ones, and in order for him to stay in the NHL it has to be the other way around.

"He is a big guy and can really body check. But he has to learn to take out his man and then go on about his own business. Sure I have faith in his potential. So do the clubs I have turned down. They want to deal for Goldy. But he has got to start putting something on the record sheet."

Through the exhibition season, Goldy was the Stars' leading goal scorer, and he was moving toward the opening face-off of that third campaign like a man ready to put something besides penalty minutes on the record sheet.

All through that training camp left winger J.P. Parise and center Ray Cullen had constantly been after Goldy to stop retaliating so quickly, and their vigilance in this matter would be rewarded.

When the Stars had returned to the Twin Cities for the start of the regular season, Parise and Cullen took Goldy out for dinner one night.

"We want you on our line," said the blunt Frenchman, Parise, "but if you want to be foolish and get more misconduct penalties, you will probably end up with a 10-goal season."

Cullen, who was to center the line for J.P. and Goldy, concurred with the Frenchman. They could, he said, have a good season if Goldy would restrain his temper and stay out of the penalty box.

Ironically, Cullen, who had worked hard to have Goldy control his anger, would not be between him and the Frenchman when they both had great seasons. Their center from early in the season would be the flighty, spirited Tommy Williams, who didn't really want to come home to Minnesota but who played as though it were an adventure he had long dreamed of.

The Stars opened the 1969-70 season with a 4-3 loss to the New York Rangers, with Goldy scoring once, as he had in the opener the previous year. But this time there would be no fading into oblivion, no Christmas season in Memphis, no penalty minutes record.

With Goldy and the fleet Danny Grant both providing consistent scoring punch, the North Stars were undergoing a metamorphosis. Where they had been prostrate before the Eastern establishment the previous year, winning only four of 36 contests, they were a source of irritation to the old clubs this time around. In their first six games against the East they were but one victory short of their entire success the previous year, winning three, losing two and tying one.

When they played the Red Wings to a 2-2 standoff at one point in the season, they established a record of success against the East by extending their string of games without a loss to six.

Their greatest accomplishment early in that third season was a 4-3 win over the Stanley Cup Champion Montreal Canadiens at Montreal, where they had not won a game in the first two years of their existence. The Stars had gone into the third period of that game trailing 3-1, and had tied it up on a goal by Goldy. Ray Cullen fired the winning goal past defenseman Ted Harris and the ageless Gump Worsley, both of whom would, a year later, play large roles in the Stars' dramatic quest for the Stanley Cup.

Quite out of character, Goldy was scoring consistently and was not dashing about the ice in a random way to mete out retribution to those who took a run at him. To be sure, there were still plenty of guys out there trying to get him off the ice, especially now that he held a hot hand. But things were going too well, for both him and his linemates, to spoil it with unruly conduct.

There were other influences as well. He had developed close personal friendships with both Parise and Williams, and the tough but congenial Frenchman served as a steadying influence, while Tommy worked at building Goldy's confidence.

After a particularly good game, Goldy had given credit for his performance to Tommy. Williams took him aside after the game and said, "Look, Goldy, you may think I'm the only center ice man you can play with now, but you're crazy. You can play this way with anyone, and you can be just as good as you want to be."

Later, Tommy, who was never known for being discreet when he had an opinion to voice, described his right wing as "the best right winger in the NHL right now."

That Goldy was cutting down dramatically on the "cheap" penalties may have been due, in part, to the fact that people were having a hard time catching up to him to commit an offense that would call for retaliation. Because that line, which became known as the Beantown Express in that all three had come out of the Boston organization, was always on the move.

St. Louis Coach Scotty Bowman, after his team had been run over by the Express, observed:

"Those three guys murdered us. They have all the makings of a very outstanding unit. J.P. is great in the corners. Goldy has that big shot. And Williams can really handle and wheel with that puck. Most important, they all move up and down the rink at about the same speed, which was fast — very fast — against us."

As Wren Blair had predicted back in Haliburton that September, it was the year for Goldy. Everything was falling in place and when that happens, even luck seems to have a way of working

for you. In a game against the Chicago Black Hawks
at Met Sports Center, Goldy, who had never been
able to put so much as a scuff on the hide of a big,
slow-moving softball with his mighty swings, swatted
at a puck in mid-air and drove it past goalie Tony
Esposito for the winning goal.

"I don't think I ever hit a baseball that good," said
the grinning winger after the game. "Danny Grant
had shot from the left point and Esposito made the
save, but he sort of bobbled the puck and let it get
away from him. I just skated by and swatted at it with
my stick blade about waist high."

Before the capacity crowd had finished ex-
pressing its glee over that accomplishment, Goldy
had raced back into the Black Hawks' zone following
the ensuing face-off, and this time fired a bullet past
Esposito. The two goals, just eleven seconds apart,
went into the club record book.

Goldy got his first NHL hat trick that season
against St. Louis, and when he met June outside the
arena after the game he said, "I'm only eighteen hat
tricks behind Gordy Howe."

By mid-season, Goldy had eighteen goals, more
than his production for the entire season in each of
the previous two campaigns, and he was voted to the
first team of the West Division All Stars. The other
five on the starting lineup were from St. Louis.

It would not be entirely a season of serenity for
Goldy. When the Stars ended a 13-game winless
streak with a 5-2 victory over St. Louis, it was feared
that Goldy's willingness to brawl may have cost the
team his services. He got into a shoving match with
Bob Plager, and this turned into a donnybrook.

When it was broken up, Goldy's hand was swollen, and there was concern that it was fractured. An X-ray revealed no break.

"It was a typical Bob Plager fight," he said later. "We got into a shoving match in the corner. I pushed him a little and then he hit me from the side. I went after him, punched him in the jaw and hurt my hand. He must be made of stone. I hit him with a pretty good one, but from the looks of my hand I got the worst of it."

Then there was the raspberry shirt.

"Why don't you buy that shirt, it would be beautiful with your grey suit?" said June, while they were shopping one day.

"That would look sharp," Goldy agreed. So he bought the raspberry-colored shirt.

A curse hung over that shirt. Every time Goldy wore it to a game, home or away, he seemed to become engaged in a brawl and came out of it with a shiner. After a game on the road, the players always looked for an out-of-the-way eating place to enjoy a quiet dinner without attracting attention, but hecklers seemed to find them no matter where they went. That raspberry shirt made it even easier for the hecklers.

When Goldy came home from a road trip with a big shiner, he pulled the raspberry shirt from his suitcase and handed it to June.

"Here, take the shirt. I don't want to see it anymore."

Goldy had a couple of memorable fights on the ice that season, memorable because his fight strategy had backfired. During a scuffle in Montreal he had tried to hold off the man nearest him by grabbing the shoulder pads of his right arm, thereby preventing him from throwing a right. The opponent was left-handed. Goldy came home with another black eye. The same thing happened in another game, only this time Goldy was knocked on his posterior.

"How did it happen this time?" asked June, when he had returned home.

"Well, you see, I didn't know this guy was left-handed. Unfortunately, you can't stop in the middle of things and ask them, 'Excuse me, but are you left-handed or right-handed?' "

Goldy had theorized before that season that unnecessary penalties may have been costing him as many as ten goals a year. If he was getting a hundred minutes of such penalties, he was missing the equivalent of 40 to 50 shifts on the ice. Furthermore, if he could avoid retaliation when an opponent had committed an obvious infraction against him, the Stars would have the power play advantage rather than both teams skating a man short.

As it worked out, the blonde bomber finished the 1969-70 season with 36 goals and 29 assists for 65 points, and lost no respect because he wasn't dashing hither and yon over the ice seeking justice for offenses committed against him. He was assessed 89 minutes in penalties, but on many of these he took an opponent to the penalty box with him.

"Maybe I'm getting away with a lot more now," Goldy said with a smile, after that season. "I'm getting a little older and wiser. Instead of striking back out in the open, you learn to hide it a little bit. Everybody does that. But most important, if somebody takes a shot at me now, I try to hold my temper. Still, there are times when I may fight with a good friend, because on the ice we're competitors.

"I chummed around with Derek Sanderson quite a bit when we were both at Niagara Falls in Junior A, and we were pretty close to each other. But when we're out there on the ice on opposite sides I'll knock him down and he'll knock me down. When he kills penalties and I'm on the power play, I'll carry the puck up the ice and laugh at him when he tries to check me. We play a cat and mouse type of thing, but I try not to let him get too close to me because he'll check me. He's a good competitor and a real hard-nosed guy."

The 36 goals not only established a team record but also made Goldy the leading goal scorer among all right wingers in the National Hockey League that season. That was not a small achievement, since he had to beat such guys as Ken Hodge, John McKenzie, Rod Gilbert, Jim Pappin, and Yvan Cournoyer, as well as Gordy Howe, that ageless right wing of the Detroit Red Wings who seven-year-old Bill Goldsworthy had chosen as his idol many years before in Kitchener.

As before, the Stars struggled right to the end of the season for a playoff berth. A four-game winning streak propelled them from fifth to third place, and that is where they finished. In the final game of the regular season, a 5-1 win over Pittsburgh, Goldy got his 36th goal to eclipse the club record of 35 set by Wayne Connelly the first season.

This time the Stars drew their arch-rivals, the St. Louis Blues, for the first round of the Stanley Cup playoffs, but it was not a repeat of that dramatic seven-game series two years before, in which four games were decided in sudden death overtime. The Blues, using intimidation as their biggest weapon, whipped the Stars in six games.

Down by two games at the outset, Minnesota revved up its Beantown Express in the third and beat the Blues, 4-2. Goldy's two third-period scores broke the contest open. The second of these was set up on a suicide play by the unselfish Tommy Williams. Wheeling with the puck at center ice, Tommy raced down the left side past several St. Louis defenders, with Goldy trailing on the right. Tommy, still going full speed, carried the puck past the goal, and ignoring the oncharging Barclay Plager, a burly and bruising defenseman, sent a perfect pass out front to Goldy before being laminated to the boards.

They were still in the thick of things when they won the fourth game, 4-0, to even the series. But then they died. The Blues took the next two games, and season number three ended for the North Stars.

Goldy had fulfilled a promise. So many people had said for so long he had within him the stuff of which greatness is made, and though he had not achieved greatness as a hockey player in just that one season, he had conquered the thing within himself that had always held him back. This was greatness.

This, not the 36 goals, not the 89 minutes in the penalty box, this, the thing or things that had held him back were gone. Goldy had finally resigned from the Falcons.

Credit Wren Blair, who never gave up on him. Credit Ray Cullen, who was not even on the same line from early in the season. Credit J.P., that hard-digging forward out of Smooth Rock Falls, Ontario, who was always more interested in winning than in personal glory. Credit Tommy Williams.

The Beantown Express had made a mark on the NHL. There was only one other line in the entire league that had scored more points: Howe, Mahovlich and Delvecchio. They had accumulated 207 points. Goldy, J.P. and Tommy had collected 204.

J.P. had his best scoring year, with 24 goals and 48 assists for 72 points — tops on the club, second best in the West Division, and tied for seventh in the NHL.

Tommy put 67 points in the record books on 15 goals and 52 assists, his best total in his nine years in the league.

One wit had speculated before that third season that the Goldy Shuffle had gone the way of the Big Apple and the Charleston, but he had not been out on that golf course near Haliburton with that young man wrapped in chains.

In addition to his superb condition, Goldy had something else going for him in that big third season of the North Stars. This was a center ice man with long, flying hair, who skated like a demon, tirelessly, with carefree abandon.

Tommy Williams had come home.

Chapter IX

Tommy

Rip Williams played hockey with one hand. That was all he had. But his love for the game was so great that he used to tape a glove on his left arm where he didn't have a hand, and then tape the glove to his stick. In that fashion Rip went out and played. If he would not make a name in the hockey world himself, he held out hope that someday one of his boys would. The second eldest of these was Tommy Williams, who was so fast on skates as a youngster that he was always playing in leagues with older kids.

More important was the fact that Rip convinced his son to forego the glories that would have been his if he had played high school hockey in his home town of Duluth, Minnesota. High school hockey players in this state play only 20 to 25 games a year.

In Canada, which does not have high school hockey but rather the Junior A and Junior B system, teen-agers play 50 to 60 games a year. To the Canadian boy hockey is not just a sport; it is a way of life.

That's the way it would be for Tommy. Free of the restrictions associated with high school hockey in

Minnesota, he could play wherever and whenever he wanted to, and he was so good that he was in much demand in the amateur system.

American hockey players are not entirely overlooked by the professional system, even though few Americans have made it to the NHL in its long history.

The pros knew about Tommy. The Boston Bruins had been in touch with him as he was coming out of Central High School, and at first he had decided to give the Canadian system a try. But he also was getting attractive offers from colleges and universities, and he feared that if he could not make it in the Canadian semi-pro system, he would not be able to come back and get one of those scholarships. He decided against the system.

Wren Blair was on his way to Kingston in the fall of 1959, to open a training camp there when the word came down that Tommy wasn't going to camp.

The Bird telephoned the Bruin front office.

"Holy God, we can't lose that kid," said Blair. "I'm going to Duluth to talk to him, and if you don't want to pay my expenses, I'll pay for them myself."

The Bird took a train from Toronto to Fort Williams, rented a car there and drove to Duluth.

"I'm sorry, I just don't want to lose my eligibility for a scholarship," Tommy told him.

"But you can make it," said The Bird.

"What if I don't?"

"I'll tell you what to do. Why don't you come to camp with us and pay your own way? We won't give you anything in the way of money. But we will give you an honest appraisal of your abilities. If you're not good enough to be a pro, we'll just tell you, and you can come back and go to college. If you make it and are satisfied with the offer, we'll reimburse you for the camp."

Tommy agreed.

When that training camp was over, the Canadians were sold on Tommy and he was ready to make a run at the big time. His apprenticeship before getting there would be short. He played part of two seasons under The Bird at Kingston in the Eastern Professional Hockey League. Midway in the second year he was called up to Boston, and there he stayed for seven years.

Tommy and his wife fell in love with Boston. Once during his years there Hap Emms, then general manager of the Bruins, wanted to send him to the minors.

Tommy wouldn't go. It was as simple as that. So Emms kept him, and in the first game he played after that he scored two goals and had two assists in a 5-4 win over Montreal. That's how bad he wanted to stay in Boston.

He didn't though. The Bruins dealt him to the North Stars in the summer of 1969, after he had sat out most of the previous season with a knee injury. There was speculation that the injury would end his career.

Tommy was playing the off wing (a right-handed shooter, he was playing the left side) when he got a pass from the Bruins' Dallas Smith. The pass was slightly behind him and he had to turn to get it. But as he turned he kept skating, and a Chicago Black Hawk caught him across the knees with a hard check. All the ligaments in one knee were torn, and later he had a ligament transplant.

Throughout his career there had been people who said Tommy Williams was not dedicated to hockey, because he was a free spirit, full of pranks and mischief, and he did not seem to take the game in the somber, dignified manner befitting a major leaguer.

His pranks and jokes in the locker room were a source of irritation to some, and a tension-reliever to others. But behind that facade was a young man as intense in his dedication to the sport as his detractors.

Tommy proved it after that serious knee injury, when the odds on his making a big comeback were crummy. He lifted weights, ran, rode a bicycle, played 27 holes of golf a day and gave that damaged limb such a working over that he gained four inches in his thigh muscles.

Whether it was his conduct off the ice, or the fear that he could not possibly make a comeback, or a combination of these things, the Bruins unloaded him.

Tommy did not want to come home.

To the people back in Minnesota it seemed like the perfect trade. A native son, one of the few ever to hack it with the big time in hockey, was coming home to play for the North Stars. This pleased them, and, therefore, it should have been a great delight to Tommy.

"I never wanted to be traded to Minnesota," Tommy said later. "I felt terrible. I felt awful. My wife cried her heart out. You wouldn't believe it. It was such a disappointing thing. Boston is head and shoulders over Minnesota for excitement, but maybe they've got the best team in the world, too.

"But what are you going to do? What are you going to do if you come into the Twin Cities and you have a press conference? Can you tell them 'God, I didn't want to be traded.' It wouldn't look too good. So I said, 'I'm very happy to be here in Minnesota,' and that kind of song and dance, and all of it was a bunch of baloney.

"But I said to myself, 'Hey, you're starting off with a new team and your knee is a question, so you better keep your mouth shut and not get the fans and writers against you, so just keep quiet.' "

That was never Tommy Williams' style. But while controlling his tongue was a remarkable achievement, so was his comeback after that knee operation. Once before, for a very few games back in Boston, Tommy had been on the ice with a big blonde kid from Kitchener, Ontario, that time as the opposite wing. Through his career he had been a winger, except for a brief time at Kingston when Wren Blair had used him at center. When the Stars opened their third season, with The Bird again behind the bench, they lacked that one consistent scoring line that every team likes to have. Impressed with Tommy's speed and playmaking abilities, Blair decided to use him at center between Goldy and Parise, both very fast.

Few lines are successful until they have gone through a period of adjustment in which the three attackers — the two wings and their center — learn to time their moves with one another. Tommy, Goldy and J.P. became a scoring machine literally overnight.

Tommy was the perfect complement to the flamboyant style of the Frenchman and Goldy, because he was one of the swiftest skaters in the NHL and could carry the puck with finesse into the attack zone. He was what old timers called a "river skater," because he roamed the ice in pursuit of the puck.

He had superb instincts and, like a master chess player, seemed to visualize the flow of the play even before it had developed. Consequently, he often flew into the face of the opposition's attack to steal the puck and start a rush back the other way.

With Tommy steaming in on his left and setting him up, Goldy began to put goals in the scorebook. When the 1969-70 season was half gone, he had been voted to the West Division All-Star team, and he was convinced that his big season was due largely to Tommy. He made a point of saying so:

"Tommy is one heck of a hockey player, and if he ever wanted to settle down and really concentrate on hockey, he'd be on this All-Star team too. He can skate and he has a good shot, but he won't shoot enough. I think his biggest asset is that he anticipates a lot. He seems to be able to project just how the play is going to flow, and then he's right there in position to take advantage of it.

"With his ability to operate around the nets he

can deke a goalie out and then pass off so J.P. or I have an open net. He doesn't care who scores. That's why he's so great."

While Tommy was the engineer of the Beantown Express, J.P. was the tireless fireman, bulldozing the puck down the boards, digging it out of the corners and setting up his linemates. Considered one of the strongest cornermen in the game, he was also one of the most durable. "Jeep," as he was called by his teammates, missed only two games in more than two and a half seasons with the Stars.

Goldy was the engine of the Express, a powerful, dynamic piece of machinery in action, and he had gained a big measure of control over himself so that he was not running recklessly over everyone in sight.

Tommy would shun off the credit people were giving him for Goldy's success:

"You know, as far as I'm concerned Goldy is one of the best players in this whole league. If he were with the Bruins now, he'd be a potential 50-goal scorer. I'm not kidding. Maybe more. Put him on Esposito's line for example. I'd say he'd score 50. He's that good.

"I think Goldy's biggest drawback, originally, was his own lack of confidence. He may have said I helped him build up this confidence, but I don't know. Maybe I helped him a little, but I'll tell you something. It doesn't come from any one person. It must be within yourself. I think maybe he saw that I acted a little reckless. I never really worried much about things and maybe he figured, what the heck, if that guy can do it, so can I. I think he found out. When he's skating, he's unbeatable."

The Express would not be running long, just one season, and then it broke down. Because Tommy was injured at the outset of the 1970-71 season, and this was the beginning of a chain of events that ended tragically and emotionally upsetting for the carefree prankster out of Duluth.

While their center ice man was trying to cure a back injury, Goldy and J.P. were being shuffled about by new coach Jack Gordon who, as Blair before him, was searching for the best combination to build a consistent scoring line. The shuffling continued through the early stages of that fourth season, and all three members of the former Beantown Express felt the impact of the changes.

Goldy was not scoring. J.P. was also well off his scoring pace of the previous season. Tommy was fretting over his ailing back and the fact that Gordon had to try other people in his role as the playmaking center for the second highest scoring line in the NHL.

When Tommy's back finally came around, with the help of cortisone treatments, he was not immediately inserted between Goldy and J.P. Gordon said he wanted him 100% before reuniting the line. It was early November before that happened, and Goldy was in the throes of a miserable scoring slump.

Just two nights before the Beantown Express was re-assembled, Tommy and his wife had gone to Goldy's house to visit him and June.

The hockey fraternity is known to be close knit, but Tommy had never been especially involved, socially, with his teammates, either at Boston or Minnesota. Nor had his wife, Emmy, been close friends with other hockey wives. Tommy preferred it that way, to have friends outside hockey, because when he was not playing he wanted to forget about the game and talk about something else. But Tommy felt close to his big blonde winger of the previous year, and sympathized with his miseries.

"Em, we're going to go buy a bucket of Kentucky Fried chicken, and go over to Goldy's house," Tommy told his wife that night. "We've just got to get him to let his hair down a little bit, have a good time and talk over his problems."

They stayed until two in the morning, talking, laughing, having that good time Tommy wanted them to have, and then he and Emmy left. That was the last time June and Goldy saw Emmy. She died of asphyxiation two nights later, the same night that the Beantown Express was put back in operation.

Tommy's troubles mounted after that, and the Express never got into high gear. Within a matter of weeks the line was benched by Coach Gordon, and it would not play together again. Tommy was not around long after that. The North Stars had a new coach with a new system and a new style in terms of attitude and team morale and deportment. Tommy wasn't adjusting to this, and Jack Gordon could not adjust his system for Tommy. They had a personality conflict.

"I want an honest answer," said Wren Blair, when he called his coach into his office, "would you feel better off with this team if Tommy weren't here?"

"Wren, I know how you've worked to build this team," said Gordon, "and I feel terrible coming in here new and causing you to lose somebody. But now that you have asked I'll have to say yes, I think it would be better for the team."

"Okay, then I'm going to trade Tommy."

The decision would cause much pain and open many wounds.

Jack Gordon issued a brief statement: "I can't have one set of rules for the team and another set for an individual. I'm truly sorry it turned out this way, but I cannot tolerate insubordination on the team."

The Bird, who had once made that long train trip to convince a kid from Duluth to come play for him, called Tommy into his office. After they talked about the trade, The Bird looked at the handsome, outspoken young man and said: "I want to thank you for the fine season you gave us last year and I want you to know I have great respect for your ability as a hockey player. But I have to back my coach in this."

Tommy went off to Oakland. In less than two years from being uprooted from Boston, which he and his wife had loved so much, he was almost as far away from there as he could get and still play in the NHL.

Whether due to the painful series of events or the fact that he simply could not be discreet when he had something on his mind, Tommy fired a blast at the North Stars from Oakland. He was quoted in newspapers from coast to coast as claiming he was railroaded to Cleveland, the Stars' farm club, just before the trade. He also said some things uncomplimentary of Coach Gordon.

This latter action brought a response from the

North Star players, who sent a telegram to a Toronto newspaper that had printed Tommy's opinions.

In it they said Gordon's behavior "warrants the respect and pride we feel for this man. The North Stars always have been treated as gentlemen and wished their true feelings could be made known."

Since everyone else was then getting into the fray, North Star president Walter Bush issued a statement about the players' statement about Tommy's statement:

"It's a tremendous tribute to our organization for the players to send a night letter like that."

The following summer Tommy met The Bird at a celebrity golf tournament sponsored by Howard Wong, who operates a fancy Cantonese restaurant only a fortune cookie throw from Met Sports Center.

"I didn't say everything those newspapers printed," said Tommy.

"You never could keep your mouth shut, so forget it," said The Bird. "I'm not interested."

"Oh, Lord, am I glad to hear that. I've been dreading this day!"

By the time Tommy got into troubled waters with management, Goldy had discovered that his former center had been right. He, Goldy, could play without Tommy centering for him, because he was having a sensational second half on a line with Danny Grant and Jude Drouin.

While Tommy's departure was a personal loss to Goldy, the latter viewed the trade with frankness:

"Considering all the circumstances, it was the

best thing, I think, for everyone concerned. Tommy and The Bird got along well. Tom respected Wren and Wren thought highly of Tommy's hockey abilities. People talk a lot about Wren and his trading, but he doesn't trade simply because he dislikes people. I think he really and truly helped Tommy by trading him.

"I can't possibly see how Tommy could have stayed here in the Twin Cities after all that happened and still play great hockey. I think it was the best thing for him to get out of the surroundings where he and his wife had their home and their friends.

"Wren tried to help him so much. I don't think he got rid of him because of what he said. I think he did this for Tommy's benefit. I hope Tommy realizes this and gets off to a fresh start."

Tommy played well for Oakland in the final weeks of that season, getting seven goals and 10 assists for 17 points in the last 18 games.

He faced his old North Star teammates once near season's end, with Oakland winning, 4-1. After the game, Goldy and J.P. went out with their former center.

"Tommy, you know how I feel about this deal," said Goldy, "I feel just terrible. But now you're doing so well out here, so why don't you quit popping off and just play hockey?"

It was ironic, that kind of advice coming from someone who had always carried his own bag full of trouble along with him. But Goldy was a different man then than he had been before Tommy had come home from Boston. Tommy, if he had trouble

growing to his own full measure of maturity, was an
instrument in helping Goldy to do so, and this Goldy
would always respect him for.

"Tommy's really a super guy as far as I'm concerned," Goldy said. "He gave me all the confidence
in the world. He always kept telling me, 'Sure I've
helped you out a bit, but you don't need me. You can
go out and score thirty goals on your own playing
with anybody.' This really built up my confidence.

"Sure, he got in trouble and said some things he
shouldn't have. But here he was, injured at the
beginning of the season, and then he wasn't playing
and he was worried and upset, and then his wife died.
It was a tough situation. I tried to talk with him and
help him out, but I guess he couldn't accept the fact
that all those things were happening. Then there was
the deadline before trading, and he knew he was on
the block.

"Tommy did a lot of popping off, perhaps too
much. I don't entirely believe in doing this. I don't
believe in burning bridges behind me, because some
day I may be coming back this way and won't be able
to come across. But Tommy's always been a bit
stubborn . . . like me at times. And if you have a
stubborn streak, you just don't want to forget things.
Then when you want to get something off your chest,
I suppose you should go talk to a wall. But if you're
Tommy Williams the wall is umpteen million sports
writers and all of a sudden you're being quoted from
coast to coast.

"I really think a lot of Tommy, and despite his
fun-loving nature, he is a very sentimental fellow.

He's outgoing in many ways, but he's a lot different when we talk about serious things.

"Perhaps the best thing about Tommy's situation, for all concerned, is to forget about it now. We all say things at times that we wish we wouldn't have."

Tommy would not forget. It wasn't his way. And when that 1970-71 season was done with, he looked back and remembered and said the things that were on his mind, as he usually did:

"I don't think I should have played in Minnesota. We wanted to stay in Boston so bad. We had all our friends out there. Possibly I'll end up living out there some time. We met a lot of people there and they were really good to us. It's probably similar to the fact that Goldy and June like it so well in the Twin Cities. For Goldy it's the first NHL team he's really made it with. He didn't play in Boston long enough to appreciate the city.

"As far as that last year in Minnesota is concerned, that was a tough deal, with my wife dying and all. You can't appreciate it until it happens. I'm not feeling sorry for myself, but you should know. Here I am, a guy with five kids and I don't know what I'm going to do about having somebody care for them. Then I still had a job to do, but I was having troubles with the coach. I tried my hardest. I think I gave them good solid performances.

"They were shuffling me around, playing all different positions, and I never complained. All I wanted to do was get out there. Then somebody started talking about me having a drinking problem. I drank, but I didn't hide it. I'm not going to sit in a corner and drink by myself, or then I will have a problem. I'd go out and have a good time and I was still playing good hockey. But I never asked anybody to come with.

"The only guy that ever went with me was Danny O'Shea and Danny's a pretty mature guy who knows how to handle his own situation. One of the younger players used to bug me to go with him, and I'd say, 'Hey, kid, you just go and behave yourself. Never mind, you don't want to follow my act.'

"I was bitter about a lot of things when I was traded, but I wasn't bitter at Blair. He's done a lot for me in my career. He felt bad about sending me to Oakland, I'm sure he did. We had spent a lot of time together.

"Sure I should have been a little more discreet on some occasions. But I'll tell you something, the pressure got to me that last year in Minnesota. The pressure was really bad. Sometimes I'd get mad because of what happened to my wife and I'd take it out on anybody that was there.

"I don't want to look for sympathy. I don't want that. I wanted something to happen that couldn't possibly happen. I wanted my wife back."

Chapter X

The Pied Piper of Haliburton

"I'm going to write you one last letter and then I won't bother you until training camp," said Finnie, a tear trickling down her cheek.

Goldy smiled at the 11-year-old and said, "Okay, and you have a good summer, hear?"

Her head bobbed up and down, however lightly, her dark hair dancing around her face.

Finnie had adopted Goldy. It is not easy for an 11-year-old who has adopted someone to give him up for several months. Even before that big third season, when he had been struggling through the bad times, Finnie had stuck with Goldy. The Bird didn't have any more faith in the handsome blonde winger than that little girl, and he definitely did not talk to Goldy in the same way or give him the same kind of presents.

Finnie's friends never had a hard time finding her among the throng at the Met. She was the only one off the ice wearing a North Star jersey with the number 8 on it.

When the other number 8 comes down the ramp from the locker room to the rink, Finnie is usually there waiting for him.

145

"I've brought you a stick of gum," she will say.

"Hey, that's great. Thank you very much," says Goldy.

Goldy goes out on the ice and skates over to the left side to start taking practice shots. That has always been a superstition with him. He starts from the left and works his way over to the right.

Finnie races down the aisles and around the rink to the other side where he is taking his shots.

"Good luck, you're going to get a goal tonight," she calls out to him.

"I hope you're right. I'll try for you."

Sometimes Finnie is with her girl friend, who wears a North Star jersey with number 30 on it, Cesare Maniago's number.

Often when Goldy went out for a public appearance, Finnie would be there waiting for him, wearing her North Star jersey.

Once a week during the season she wrote him a letter, always enclosing a stick of gum. And then she would be there at the next home game as he came down that ramp.

"Did you get my letter?"

Goldy smiled at her and said, "You wait here, I got a little something for you." Then he skated over and got a puck with the North Star crest on it, put a piece of white tape on the back, wrote on the tape, and skated back to where she was waiting.

"Here, this is for you."

The inscription said: "To my girl, Finnie, from Goldy."

Once while he was on the ice and they were talking back and forth Goldy said, "When you get a little older, you can baby sit for us."

After one game Finnie was still there by the time Goldy had dressed, and he introduced her to his wife, June. The little girl was very shy until Goldy told June, "We're going to have Finnie baby sit our next child."

Finnie grinned, nodded her head proudly, and said, "Yup, that's what I'm going to do."

Sometimes when Goldy and June were walking together at a game, Finnie would walk beside them. Goldy would put his arm around the child, and her face would be one large smile.

If Goldy could not seem to avoid running into people on the ice, he never tried to avoid them off the ice. Win or lose, he always came out the same door. It didn't matter whether he was feeling the pleasure of victory or the sting of defeat, or the frustration of a mediocre performance — he would not avoid that public, which can be outrageously fickle at times.

Although some of his peers in hockey and other sports occasionally use clever means to elude the people who are milling around outside the gates, Goldy felt that if they waited all that time to see him then it was only right for him not to disappoint them.

After every home game he would meet June outside the dressing room where the wives, family friends, business associates and others waited for the players. Then they would go up the south hall of the basement at the Met and out the door by the west truck ramp. There, inevitably, they would encounter a group of people — mostly youngsters — lined up along the walkway paralleling the truck ramp and standing at the fringe of the parking lot. The size of the crowd often depended on the weather, which, in a Minnesota winter, is usually described in one of two ways: bad and terrible.

Sometimes people waited there in temperatures well below zero, so their children could get an autograph from one of their idols. They had to wait 45 minutes to an hour, if their hero was the Stars' blonde right wing. Goldy is a notoriously slow dresser, and is usually the last player out.

"Since I'm usually last out," he said, "I figure those people have waited a long time, often in such cold weather, just for an autograph, so I'm going to cooperate.

"Maybe some guys have personal reasons for evading the fans, or maybe they're embarrassed about facing the public after they've played a bad game. But shucks, if you've had a bad game, you've had a bad game. That's it. Most people are pretty nice about it."

Sometimes they are not nice about it, but even the possibility of facing the hecklers does not cause Goldy to change course. Fans, friendly or hostile, pay his salary. And back in those days in the minors at Oklahoma City he was never sure when he came out the door if he would be patted on the back or punched in the nose. It all depended on what town they were playing in and who was waiting out there after the game. So he had developed a tolerance for whatever would come.

One thing he could not do was walk past a kid with a pen and paper in his hand.

"Even if we're a bit rushed for time, or if I'm hungrier than a horse, I'll make time. Look at it this way: maybe the autographing takes an extra few minutes. That means it's like hitting two or three extra stop lights on the way to getting something to eat after a game. That's really all it takes."

Because of his hard-hitting, sometimes reckless style of play, Goldy had attracted a following in his first years with the North Stars. It seemed that people wanted either to sprinkle him with affection or deluge him with anger. The friendly ones included Finnie; another youngster who formed a fan club because he liked the way Goldy fought; the paper boy; a couple of young girls who planted a tree in his honor in Israel, and assorted others, most of them young people. Then there were The Bird, Clarence Campbell, and a whole stable of hockey watchers who thought Goldy was too cantankerous to ever be a major leaguer and should be traded away.

The balance between his devotees and detractors shifted dramatically after that 36-goal third season. Suddenly he was in demand everywhere, by all kinds of people. In the months between the end of the third season and the start of the fourth, he did not see June and Tammy much more than he had when the Stars were in action and traveling around the country.

He went back to Haliburton for one month, to that place on the edge of the Ontario wilderness where he had tortured his body only a year earlier on that bumpy little golf course, and there he again instructed youngsters coming to the Haliburton Hockey Haven.

"Goldy was the best instructor we had," said Wren Blair, who operates that hockey camp. "A lot of guys would go on the ice and check to see who the women are in the seats. Goldy was all business. He spent a lot of time with the kids, individually, showing them how to do things and keeping them in a good frame of mind.

"He's like the Pied Piper. When he skated out on the rink he would have 17 billion kids following him."

Early one morning Goldy had the duty with a group of 40 seven-year-old boys. It is cold in Haliburton in the early morning hours, but he herded them out onto the ice. All but one. Goldy was leading the kids in skating drills when he noticed a nose poking out over the boards by the bench. The nose belonged to a small boy, Peter Yonkovich, who was sitting there watching the drill, not trying to hide as some youngsters did when they couldn't get going early in the morning. Goldy waved to him. Peter waved back. Goldy skated over.

"Hey, Pete, how are you doing this morning?"

Peter looked at him sleepily.

"You know, your parents have paid good money figuring you'd learn something here. Don't you think you should be out here with your buddies, learning proper fundamentals of skating?"

"Well, Mr. Goldsworthy, it's not that I don't want to skate, it's my feet that don't want to skate today."

Some kids got hurt and cut at that camp, for the first time in a hockey game, and they'd be scared when they were hauled off to the local hospital for stitches.

"Aw heck, that's nothing," Goldy would tell the frightened youngster, "you take a couple of stitches and go back and show those other guys and you'll be king of the castle."

"Will I?"

"Darn right."

When the stitches were in, Goldy would take the lad to a mirror.

"See that? You go back and show those guys."

Later the wounded warrior would be seen skating all over the rink saying, "Hey, look what I got!" It was a badge of honor.

When Goldy returned to the Twin Cities that summer of 1970, he considered the possibility of having the telephone taken out of his home.

"When I was scoring 14 goals a season I didn't have much use for it because it never rang," he said, "and then all of a sudden it's going all the time. You get all kinds of calls from people you don't know and have never heard of before, but they always have an idea where you can make a buck. You have to be very careful of these things."

He received one call that summer from a guy who had taken some money off another North Star player in a "deal" that didn't pay off.

"Hey, Goldy, I've got this sure-fire thing going where you can make a fortune with an investment of just $10,000. What do you think of that?" asked the huckster.

"That sounds great," said Goldy.

"You really can't lose on this one. How does the price sound?"

"Not bad. I'll tell you what, you show me your $10,000 and I'll show you mine."

"Okay, I'll call you back in a couple of days."

Goldy never heard from him again.

Perhaps it was the memories of his own reckless flight through life as a youngster, or that he simply trusted them more, but whatever, Goldy had a strong bond with young people. Not that he wasn't sociable with adults. He makes friends quite easily and will stand around and shoot the breeze with strangers just to show them he is not the mean, cranky guy they may think he is while he's on the ice. But he always warms up rapidly to youngsters, and they to him, and if he is talking to a group of them, he never fails to impart upon them his feelings about the importance of getting an education and of applying the 3D philosophy — desire, dedication, determination — to the things they would do in life.

They usually applied this philosophy to their interrogation of Goldy, because their questions are mostly blunt and sometimes embarrassing.

"How come you're not as good as Gordy Howe?" a kid asked him once.

"Well . . ."

"How much money do you make a year?" asked another.

"Well, Wren Blair thinks he pays me too much and I think he doesn't pay me enough, so we settle at a happy medium."

"Who do you like to fight the most?"

"Anybody I can beat. But you don't pick your fights. Most of the time there is so much tension in a game that a little thing will touch off a fight. Usually I look up to see the guy I'm paired off against and he's 6 foot-4 inches high and I say to myself, 'Oh, no, how did I get into this one?' "

Sometimes youngsters will not be put off by evasive answers.

"Who's the weakest hockey team in the NHL?" the youth asked.

Trying to be diplomatic, Goldy said, "I wouldn't say there's such a thing as a weak team. There might be a club that has bad problems. Some people say Oakland has a bad club because they ended in last place, but they may have some problems right now."

"Okay then," said the persistent lad, "which team has the most bad problems?"

Once in a discussion with a group of young boys, one of them dropped this bomb on him:

"Do you get fined if you get drunk, or if you drink?"

"Well, to be honest fellows, a lot of players like a cold beer after a game. But nobody should drink four or five cases at a time. In everything, you know, moderation is the best approach. As for me, I've got to remember I'm a pro athlete and that I should set a good example. In answer to part of your question, if the manager caught a guy as stiff as a boot, he'd probably fine him."

While the demands on Goldy for public appearances ate into much of his summer hours, he also
had an increasing load of fan mail to read.

There was, of course, the weekly letter and stick
of gum from Finnie (until her parents told her she
should stop bothering him that summer after the
playoff with Montreal), frequent, hastily scribbled
notes from the paper boy, and a variety of one-time
correspondence from other people.

Wren Blair gave Goldy a copy of a letter he had
received in that big third season, and it read:

"Dear Coach Blair: I had my first opportunity last
Saturday to see the North Stars as they triumphed
over the St. Louis Blues. It was a tremendous performance and like all the other North Star fans, I was
most pleased and excited. Will you give my greetings
and good wishes to each of the North Star players
and particularly to Bill Goldsworthy who did such a
masterful job on Saturday and to J.P. Parise who,
along with his teammates, came through with flying
colors against the Philadelphia Flyers. I hope to get
back to see the North Stars in action again. You have
a new fan, and I am a noisy and avid one."

Few would question that the gentleman would,
indeed, be a noisy fan, since the letter was signed by
Hubert Humphrey.

Along with personal appearances, Goldy began
to receive offers for endorsements of products, and
he loaned his name to a skate-manufacturing
company for promotional purposes. This he did
without reservation, since he went through three pair
of skates each season, each pair costing $70. They

are made out of kangaroo hide, and he selects them of a size that is skin tight. That is in sharp contrast to the old pair he had as a boy, in which he had to stuff a pound and a half of paper to make them fit.

Even with business opportunities beginning to come his way, and former vice presidents of the United States writing nice things about his playing abilities, and city fathers inviting him to public functions, wherever he went Goldy seemed to attract or be attracted by children.

When he went shopping with June and Tammy one day in late summer of 1970 upon returning from Haliburton, he wandered over to the magazine rack in a store and began leafing through a magazine. Then he looked down at a small boy beside him, who was looking at a hockey magazine. On the very page the boy was looking at was a photograph of Bill Goldsworthy, the North Stars' star right wing. The boy looked up at Goldy, then back at the picture in front of him. Then he turned and ran, shouting, "Mom, mom, come here!"

A short time later the boy returned, pulling his mother behind him, and he pointed at the picture and then at Goldy.

Again he had gone to the supermarket with June and he was walking down an aisle when he felt a tug on his coat. He looked over his shoulder but there was no one there, so he kept going. Another tug, and this time he turned and looked down at a child, barely bigger than a toddler, holding out a pencil and a piece of paper.

"Hi there, what's your name?" asked Goldy.

The child just stood there, mute, holding out the pencil and paper in a tiny hand. Goldy took it from him and signed his name, then handed it back to him. The child turned and galloped away, never saying a word.

While Goldy would remember these many moments, there was one letter he received that summer of his success that he carefully preserved in his scrap book:

"Dear Bill Goldsworthy (Goldy): We are two very hockey-minded fans of yours. Would you believe two sixth grade girls? Well, we're both. For girls we know pretty much about hockey. We know about many hockey players in the National Hockey League. If we were to list the names of the players we know of we wouldn't have room to tell any more. We watch you play and every article about hockey that's in the paper we cut out and post up. There is a Jewish tradition that on Jewish Arbor Day we send in money to plant a tree to honor someone. This year we are pooling our money and having one planted to honor you. We admire you like the teens admire the pop groups. Your different (or at least we hope different) fans, / s / Ellie Bach and Judy Chucker"

Chapter XI

The Big Second Half

It was almost as though he were living in the tumultuous past, and that every stride he had made to get where he was had been wiped clean from the board.

Goldy was in year four with the North Stars, but playing like year one. Or, at least the results were like year one.

Wren Blair had prophesied: "When Goldy got those 36 goals in the third year, a lot of people, including Goldy, were very surprised. I wasn't. I always knew he was capable of that. But the thing about Goldy is that he's also capable of getting ten goals. He's very easily satisfied."

When the Stars opened that fourth season, a big center named Walt McKechnie was playing between Goldy and J.P., and in the home opener at the Met, McKechnie blasted in three goals in a 4-2 victory over Pittsburgh. But that was the most notable achievement of that line, which was together only briefly.

Through the first ten games of the 1970-71 season it seemed that Blair's prophesy was like an accurate book review of a book that hadn't yet been written.

Goldy had only one goal, and he was back in the soup with Clarence Campbell, the NHL's one-man collection agency.

This was the result of a game at the Met with the New York Rangers, in which Goldy was assessed a holding penalty. Reacting in a manner that had become less typical of him, Goldy had exploded a little bit, and was rewarded with a ten minute misconduct penalty. Goldy then had a bigger explosion, with greater results. He was given a game misconduct penalty.

"I don't mind penalties as long as they're good ones," said Jack Gordon, following the incident, "but Goldy getting thrown out hurt us. I was mad at the referee, but at Bill, too, because he's too valuable a man to lose."

Campbell also was mad, and fined Goldy $150 for breaking his stick and waving it at the referee.

"I talked to Mr. Campbell on the phone," said the dejected winger, "and I was glad to get off with the $150 fine."

The season had been bad from the start, as far as Goldy was concerned, with the dynamic Tommy Williams ailing, a new coach pushing a new system, and Goldy unable to adjust to the unsettling, frequent changes being made as the Stars tried to find a combination that would give them that one solid scoring line.

J.P. also suffered an early season injury, one of the rare times the tough Frenchman was hurt bad enough to miss action.

Goldy's early season slump got worse and worse, and coming off that 36-goal season only made matters more irritating. Try as he did, the puck was not going into the net as it had a year ago. His frustration drove him to work harder, but to no avail in the matter of scoring.

There is a certain timing, or rhythm a hockey line develops, and if it becomes an instinctive thing, the line works well. Goldy and Tommy and J.P. had developed that kind of rhythm the previous year, but it would not be recaptured. When Tommy's injured back was considered 100% healed, Gordon brought the line back together in early November. But they had already lost one month of the season, as well as the training camp, and this was valuable time that could not be recovered.

And then Emmy died.

There would be no overnight rejuvenation of the past year's second highest scoring line in the NHL. J.P. was playing as he always had, like the fullback who got those three or four yards every time, working, driving, battling unselfishly for the team cause, but he had never been a prolific scorer. Tommy, if he were 100% physically, was something less than that in mental attitude, and this would fester into the bitter confrontation with management by mid-season. And Goldy, as he had in the past, was bearing the brunt of the criticism for the sad showing of his line. That is the way thoroughbreds who run only to the smart of the whip have to be treated. Even though he denied the accusations, his weight was the chief source of irritation to Gordon and

Blair. There was no consensus on just how many pounds overweight he was. It seemed to depend on who was saying it and when they said it.

After a short and unproductive reunion, the famous Beantown Express was shut down by Jack Gordon. He benched the Williams' line.

"I've said to them time and time again: I'll wait for you, you show me," said Gordon. "I haven't seen it yet. I don't want them hurting the club, and I guess it's my job to bench them. They're all good players, but they can hurt the club, too. We have to have them if this club is to win. But when things are not going well, then you just work harder."

The poor showing of the line was particularly alarming because this was a crucial year for the North Stars. The NHL had re-aligned its two divisions by moving the powerful Chicago Black Hawks into the West. It was assumed the Hawks would be the class of the West, and that the tough St. Louis Blues would easily nail down another of the playoff berths. That meant the remaining five teams in the West would have to battle for the two remaining playoff spots.

December came and it looked like another cheerless Christmas season for Goldy. At the start of the month he had gone 41 days without a goal, and the prospects of his finishing with anywhere near the 36 goals of the previous season were remote.

He did have one of those games for which he is often remembered, early in December. He broke a 17-game goal drought with a game winner, scored a one-round technical knockout over an opponent,

ON TARGET — Goldy (8) fires at St. Louis Blues' Goaltender Glenn Hall at Met Sports Center. Others from left are North Star J. P. Parise (11) with Bill McCreary and Al Arbour (3) of St. Louis.

CLASH WITH CANADIENS — Goldy (8) tangles with Larry Hillman of Montreal. At one time or another each of the players was a North Star. From left are Ted Harris, now with Minnesota; Ray Cullen, now retired; Bobby Rousseau, later with North Stars, then traded to New York; Hillman, a former North Star; Goldy, Bob McCord and Linesman John Ashley.

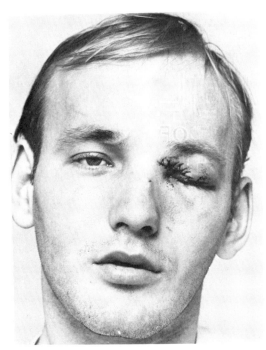

QUARTER-INCH FROM DARKNESS — Goldy came close to losing an eye after being slashed by stick in a mishap at Chicago. (Minneapolis Star Photo)

CHANGING ON THE FLY — Goldy scrambles over the boards to relieve a teammate during action at the Met. Others from left are Terry Caffery, Charlie Burns, Jude Drouin, Danny Grant (behind Goldy), Ted Hampson and J.P. Parise.

FIRST SEASON GOAL is slipped past Pittsburgh Goaltender Les Binkley by Goldy at the Met.

BAD DANCING PARTNERS — Goldy engages in a different type of shuffle with Boston's Rick Smith.

AWWRRRIGHT! The Goldy Shuffle, a carefree act of happy showmanship, was created by impulse in a game at Pittsburgh and now has become a familiar scene throughout the NHL.

DRESSED IN SUNDAY DUDS, five-year-old Bill Goldsworthy straddles pet horse at family home in Kitchener, Ontario.

GOLDY at 12 years of age.

IN FINAL YEAR OF JUNIOR A HOCKEY, Goldy worked with these instructors at a coaches' clinic in Kingston, Ontario. From left top row are Bernie Parent, Major Danny McLeod, Gilles Marotte, Dan Rope, Steve Atkinson. From left front row are Brian Bradley, Glen Sonmor, Goldy, Hap Emms, Ron Schock.

SEVERAL NHL STARS ARE ALUMNI of this Niagara Falls Junior A team. Among those pictured are Gilles Marotte, top row, second from left, now with Los Angeles; Derek Sanderson, top row, fifth from left, Boston; John Arbour, middle row, second from right, St. Louis; Bernie Parent, bottom row at left, Toronto; Goldy, bottom row, fourth from left; Ron Schock, bottom row, fifth from left, Pittsburgh; and Doug Favell, bottom row far right, Philadelphia. Hap Emms, coach and general manager, is in middle row, fifth from left. (Photo by Ron Roels, Niagara Falls)

GOLDY'S NUMBER ONE FAN — During Junior A career at Niagara Falls, Goldy met the former June Ness, who now is his wife and number one rooter. (Photo by Henry A. Simacek, Sr., Minneapolis.

GOLDY and Daughter Tammy doing Goldy Shuffle.
(Minneapolis Star Photo)

EXPLOSIVE NATURE of Bill Goldsworthy on the ice is symbolized by this sign placed by teammates at Met Sports Center lockerroom.

received a game misconduct penalty, and was fined
— all this against the California Seals. The brawl
erupted when the Stars' Tom Reid got in a fight with
a Seal player. Dennis Hextall went to the aid of his
teammate. Goldy tried to hold Hextall back, and the
latter swung at him. Goldy struck back.

"I got in a few licks and lucked out this time," said
Goldy later.

Like the spirit of Christmas seasons past,
Clarence Campbell came back to haunt Goldy. He
fined him $100 this time.

Goldy's difficulties seemed to be infectious. As
mid-season approached, the Stars were bouncing
around in the bottom half of the standings, their only
consistent scoring provided by the streaking Danny
Grant and the rookie center, Jude Drouin.

Wren Blair was perturbed, and told his coach,
Jack Gordon: "Jack, you've got to bear down on
Goldy and shake him up. He's the kind of guy you
have to keep riding or he's never going to produce,
and we need him badly."

Gordon summoned Goldy to his office several
times, and on these occasions told him: "I un-
derstand what it's like when the puck isn't going in
for you. But when that happens, you just have to
work harder at it. I have great confidence in you, and
I know everything is going to be okay if you just bear
down."

This helped Goldy keep the faith with himself
when he might have become discouraged and
depressed as in previous years when he had troubles.

Still, his difficulties in scoring were so frustrating as to be almost humorous at times.

In a game at Pittsburgh, while the Stars were on the power play, Danny Grant had taken a shot that the goalie had knocked down. Goldy was flying in unmolested to get the rebound right in front of the cage. The goalie was flat on the ice and all Goldy had to do was lift the puck gently over his legs and into the net. But, figuring the prone goaltender might try to kick a leg out, Goldy raised the puck for the roof of the net.

The puck not only did not go into the net but also it did not stay in the rink, sailing gracefully over the glass in back of the goal. Everyone on the bench was laughing as Goldy skated back shaking his head in disbelief.

"Really though," said the dejected winger, "I've never experienced anything quite like this. I'm getting at least three good chances every game but either the goalie makes a great save, or I miss the net by a hair. Well, not always a hair. Sometimes I'm missing the net while the goaltender is out for lunch."

A lot of people were diagnosing Goldy's problems in those lean days, and one diagnosis was that he was passing up clear shooting chances from the point on the power play. This Goldy disputed.

"I don't shoot from the point if there isn't a screen. I don't care if it's Bobby Hull shooting, the goalie shouldn't have much trouble saving a shot from that far out if he can see it all the way. The goalie will either deflect it out of the rink or give it to a defenseman, and then you've given up the puck. If there is a screen, I shoot low for either the right or left side, because somebody should be there to tip it in, or it might go in by itself because it's hard for the goalie to see. Somebody like Danny Grant is different, because he can thread a needle with his shot."

By the mid-season All-Star game break, Goldy had only six goals, and it was no longer a question of whether he could match his previous season's total, but whether he could even match the fourteen he had gotten in each of his first two years.

At least part of his problem stemmed from the fact that through that first half he had played with eleven different hockey players in a variety of line combinations. And while all of them were good, each had his own style and his own timing. The constant changes in the makeup of lines made it difficult to work out the timing and coordination to play effectively as a unit.

In the final game of the first half, just before the All-Star game, Goldy was knocked unconscious in a collision with Parise, and suffered a mild concussion. He would wear a helmet after that.

While the rocket-shooting Grant, who had an impressive total of twenty-one goals at mid-season, and the Stars' policeman-defenseman, Ted Harris, who had been obtained in a trade with Montreal, were playing in the All-Star game, the Minnesota brass was dreaming up new line combinations in a quest for more consistency.

Early in the second half of the season, Jack Gordon sent out a new line. On the left side was the handsome Danny Grant, whose boyish face and neatly kept dark hair gives him the appearance of a maturing choir boy. That he did not have the flair for the dramatics as other players did may have caused some North Star partisans to overlook some qualities he possesses. He can skate like the wind and the rifle shots that come off his stick are deadly accurate. He is not spectacular, he is effective, and these qualities were not overlooked by the opposition.

His center was the dashing featherweight rookie, Jude Drouin who, at 21, had not learned proper respect for the big, tough center icemen he faced off with. And while the opposition was intent upon bouncing him from to board like the steel ball in a pinball machine, the young Frenchman, his black hair flowing, was like the hound chasing the fox in his pursuit of the puck. Once he had the scent, he pursued the black missile in a reckless, roaming way, ultimately bringing it to bay and then putting it on the sticks of his blasting wings. At mid-season, he had 11 goals and 18 assists.

On his right was the inconsistent, unpredictable Goldy, who had thought after that third season that there was only one center in all of hockeydom with whom he could find success and happiness. But that was before he had skated consistently alongside Drouin, only to find that the rookie, as Tommy Williams, was a gypsy on ice, and a fast one, too.

So it was Grant, Drouin and Goldy, and this time Jack Gordon's search for a scoring line had come to an end. So did Goldy's slump. Fitted with his first helmet ever, Goldy may not have evoked the total personal identification from the spectators, as Wren

Blair had speculated, but there was no mistaking those wild charges down the right wing.

Over in Boston Phil Esposito, with a supporting cast quite unlike anything hockey had seen in a long time, was scoring at a pace that would make shambles of Bobby Hull's single season goal record. This unprecedented performance would be matched almost goal for goal by Goldy during the second half.

The Drouin-Goldy-Grant line was an overnight success, even as the Beantown Express had been the previous season, but this time the season was half gone and Goldy was a long way off his pace of a year earlier.

He did a lot of catching up, fast. He immediately went on a six-game goal scoring streak before being stopped by the Detroit Red Wings in early February. He came back with a seven-game streak, again stopped by the Wings.

Meanwhile, Drouin was on a streak of his own, in which he collected at least a goal or an assist in fifteen consecutive games.

Observing Goldy's furious pace, Parise, who had been involved in that mid-season collision, commented wryly: "He should pay me for ringing his bell."

Whether the helmet he had donned played a part in his comeback is only speculation, but Goldy did not think so.

"I don't think the helmet has anything to do with it," he said during one of his streaks. "I know it's awfully hot with that thing on. It feels like your head is in an oven.

"I've been fortunate to play these games on a line with Danny and Jude. They've been great. I'm convinced Drouin is going to be a great NHL center."

Just as they had speculated over Goldy's difficulties in the first half of the season, hockey watchers were now conjuring up all kinds of theories about his hot hand.

Only one man knew the real secret to his resurgence; Lou Nanne. Lou, like many other athletes, had a superstition. He would not go on the ice unless he followed Goldy out. At home, on the road, it didn't matter where they were, Nanne always waited for Goldy and then followed him out.

This had never bothered Goldy until that terrible scoring drought.

Goldy developed a superstition that it was Nanne following him out that was causing his scoring miseries.

He looked down the bench one night and saw that Louie was waiting for him, so he dashed into the washroom to escape him. There he stalled as long as he could, and he started back.

Lou was waiting for him.

"Hurry up, Goldy, we're going to be late."

"Louie, you've got to quit following me. All the time you're following me and I can't get any points."

"You may not be scoring, but we're winning."

"Fine, that's good. But please quit following me."

"Come on, or we're going to be late."

Later, when Goldy did start scoring, Lou was following him out one night, as always, and said to him. "See, I told you everything would be all right, didn't I?"

Twice during that big second half Goldy's scoring tempo could have been undone through problems encountered by Drouin. The rookie injured a hand in one game, but stayed in the lineup with a cast on it. If it bothered him, it did not show. In his first game with the cast, he was involved in all three goals as the Stars beat California, 3-2. Two of Minnesota's goals were made by Goldy, his 14th and 15th in his last 14 games. Over that span he broke a club record with goals in those seven consecutive games.

While nothing Goldy had blasted at the nets seemed to go in during the early part of the season, everything he threw at it was now — including a 100-foot shot in a game with Philadelphia. Down 2-1 with less than a minute to play, the Flyers had pulled their goalie in favor of a sixth skater, and they were pressuring the Stars in Minnesota's zone. Goldy intercepted a pass and fired down ice toward the open net, which was considered a risky play since if he had missed, icing would be called and the puck brought back into the Stars' zone for a face-off. The long shot skidded into the middle of the goal. It was a calculated risk on Goldy's part, since he practiced that very shot from the right side of the rink at least thirty times a day, and had gotten to where he made it seven out of ten times.

If Drouin were partly responsible for Goldy's performance, perhaps Goldy had an impact on Jude's. Right in the middle of that streak, Drouin had to sit out a three-game suspension as the result of a

fuss involving an official. He may have been reading
Goldy's press clippings.

Gordon was concerned over the potential effects
of the rookie's suspension.

"I want to keep that line intact. If Goldy can keep
drilling the puck into the twine, we'll be in the
playoffs. He has worked well with Drouin."

The suspension did nothing to break the rhythm
of the Drouin line, or to stop the rampaging Goldy.
Drouin returned to the lineup and scored a goal and
four assists in the next two games.

In mid-March of 1971, Goldy scored the hat trick
against Los Angeles, giving him 30 goals for the
season and 100 in NHL play. He also had 24 goals in
his last 27 games.

Not content with a mere hat trick, Goldy went
out the very next game, in Vancouver, and personally dismantled the first-year team with a club
record of four goals, in a 6-3 victory. That made it
seven goals in two consecutive games and 28 in his
last 28. At that point, even Esposito was not that red
hot, having gotten 25 goals in his previous 28 outings.

Wren Blair was in a sentimental mood as he
watched Goldy's assault on Vancouver by television.
Cesare Maniago was in the nets that day, for the
eighth straight game, a span in which he had won five
games and tied one.

"At no time have I ever seriously considered
trading either Goldy or Cesare," said The Bird, who
had dealt away every other player he had acquired in
the expansion draft. "I'll admit I did ask too much
from one club for Cesare, but my price was so high I

knew they would turn it down. At the end of last year I was offered a 3-for-1 deal for Goldy by an old division club. I turned it down the next day.

"I said when we drafted Goldy that he could be another Bobby Hull. He had the same style and mannerisms of Hull. We knew he had the equipment. I found when I coached that he played better under the needle. I tended to turn my head on some of the things he did early in his career. We suffered through his maturing, but I figured if he could survive me and I could survive him, he'd be great.

"Goldy has to have a centerman to get him the puck. And there's no doubt playing with Drouin has helped him. Drouin is doing what Tommy Williams did a year ago."

Toronto vice president King Clancy was in Vancouver to see Goldy's greatest goal-scoring day as a professional, and he made a brief and concise observation: "That guy has a cannon shot, and he's on the net all the time."

He would not have thought so had he been in Pittsburgh earlier in the year when Goldy stood in front of that open net and chipped the puck up over the glass like a well-stroked 9-iron shot.

The second half resurgence of the Goldy shuffle prompted his wife, June, to comment: "Maybe they should bang Bill in the head whenever he gets into a slump."

Goldy's outburst against Vancouver was the end of his incredible second half. He finished the regular season with 34 goals and 31 assists for 65 points. The only teams he had failed to score against during that streak were Detroit and Toronto, but then, he rarely scored against Toronto. The Maple Leafs' goalies, Bernie Parent and Jacques Plante, had always had a hex on Goldy.

During that stretch when he was scoring at a clip of a goal a game for 28 contests, Goldy fired a total of 139 shots, scoring at an average of once every fourth shot.

Drouin, the perpetual motion machine on skates, broke the rookie record for assists, with 52, and added 16 goals for a total of 68 points.

Grant, as always, had also been productive, matching Goldy's 34 goals and adding 23 assists.

They don't keep half-season records in the National Hockey League, which is unfortunate for Goldy. If they did, the 28 goals he produced would go down as one of the greatest efforts in the history of the league.

Chapter XII

The One Second Season

They swarmed over the Montreal blue line in one final rush, and even those though Canadiens, with their long tradition of pride and excellence at the game of hockey, could not stop these young upstarts from the West. The clock would do that.

Fifteen thousand people were on their feet screaming when Ted Hampson, a swift wing the Minnesota North Stars had acquired in a mid-season trade from the California Seals, swept across the blue line with the puck. He poised to fire on goal, but the puck had gotten in too close to him. Instead he passed ahead to Jude Drouin, the flying Frenchman right out of the Montreal chain, who had waged a brilliant battle for rookie-of-the-year honors. The puck was slightly behind Drouin and hit his skate, bounding back to Hampson. The clock said one second and the clamor of the crowd was deafening.

Montreal goalie Ken Dryden had made his move against the potential Drouin threat, and was now sprawled on the ice out of position. Hampson rifled the puck into the net.

The goal judge pushed the button on the red light, to signal the tying score. The button would not give and the light would not go on. There would be no more red lights for the North Stars in the spring of 1971. Instead, the green light, which signals the end of playing time and which automatically freezes the red one, winked at the disappointed and angry North Stars. Their long season had been one second too short.

The protest charge toward referee Bill Friday was led by the big blonde right winger of the Stars, Bill Goldsworthy, who never had been known for accepting adversity with serenity. It was to no avail. The final score would stand: Montreal 3, North Stars 2.

The Canadiens had won the semi-final series in the Stanley Cup playoffs, 4 games to 2. They would go on to defeat the Chicago Black Hawks in seven games, and Lord Stanley's Cup would return to the city it was so familiar with.

A line out of a Montreal newspaper summed up the series:

"The Canadiens boasted a wide edge in collective size, winning tradition, natural ability and reputation, but if the North Stars would only stop skating for a moment, I'm sure the entire hockey world would like to measure the size of their hearts."

Expansion hockey had started four years earlier, but it wasn't until that day in April, 1971 that it turned the corner. No one was optimistic enough to predict that an expansion team would have the personnel to claim the cup in the next few years. Certainly they were building toward parity with the established teams, but there was an element missing:

they did not have any superstars. Superstars are not made available in expansion drafts. Superstars are rarely traded, and then only for another superstar or a handful of potential superstars.

"I'll tell you this," said Wren Blair, general manager of the North Stars, following the Montreal series, "you take a team like Chicago and say to them, 'You take any two players off our club and we take any two we want off yours, and then we'll play hockey,' and we are going to play them even. They've got Bobby Hull and Stan Mikita, and that is the difference between us."

Even without superstars, the North Stars went farther than anyone dared dream in the 1970-71 season. The expansion teams had, in seventeen previous Stanley Cup playoff games with the old clubs, come away without a single victory. The 17th loss was a humiliating one. It occurred in the city of Montreal, and the victims were the Minnesota North Stars. Coming off a quarter-final series victory over St. Louis, the Stars had gone to Montreal to open a series which one expert referred to as a meeting between a band of pygmies and the Montreal giant killers.

Neither team had been expected to survive the opening round of Cup play, because the Stars drew the St. Louis Blues, who had beaten them out of two previous playoffs, and Montreal went against the Boston Bruins, who had the most fearsome attack in the history of the NHL.

Minnesota had suffered key injuries in a brutal confrontation with the hard checking Blues. In the first game of the series, Goldy had taken a crunching check from defenseman Bob Plager, whose low hits have been challenged as being illegal. Goldy suffered a pulled muscle, and did not return to the lineup until the start of the Montreal series. More critical, in terms of the Stars' series with the Canadiens, was the loss of defenseman Doug Mohns, who had been acquired in a mid-season trade with Chicago. Mohns was also swept off his skates by a low check from Plager, in the final game of the St. Louis series, and he would miss the rest of the playoffs. That was a severe blow to Minnesota's hopes, since what they needed badly against Montreal was a defenseman who could deftly carry the puck out of his own zone to launch an attack. The Canadiens' fierce forechecking made that essential.

It was that same forechecking that had led to one of the greatest upsets in modern hockey. Montreal had stunned the mighty Bruins by winning the seventh and deciding game of their playoff, and by doing it where the Bruins had been all but unbeatable the entire season: in Boston Gardens.

So, when the semi-final series opened in Montreal, the Canadiens were riding high — proud, confident, relaxed — while Minnesota was nursing some wounds. Goldy was back in the lineup, his injury mended, but the layoff took an edge off his effectiveness. Still, a writer noted after that first game: "Bill Goldsworthy, who returned to action after a lengthy layoff, tried hard and scored Minnesota's second goal late in the game, but he was like a blotter trying to stem a flood."

The Stars came out skating strongly in the first period, and Danny Grant hummed a shot past the Canadiens' giant goalie, Ken Dryden, to give Minnesota a 1-0 lead. Dryden, who stood 6-4 without skates and weighed 210 pounds, had been the hero of Montreal's series win over Boston.

The Canadiens tied the game on a goal by Mark Tardif, who would boast later that night: "Now we win in four games."

The tight opening game may have been turned around by the Stars' failure to convert a penalty shot — one of the most rare and dramatic plays in sports. Drouin's line was on the ice when the call was made against the Canadiens.

Drouin, Grant and Goldy skated to the bench while the anticipation and excitement mounted over the forthcoming event. Any North Star who had been on the ice when the call was made was eligible to take the penalty shot. Any North Star but one. Goldy disqualified himself. He remembered that time way back in the Junior A days at Niagara Falls when he had two penalty shots in one game, missing them both, and he had never wanted to be thrust into that pressure situation again.

"Give me two guys to go over, and I don't care how big they are, I'll do that, but not just that goalie," he had said once.

Jack Gordon went to the boards as the trio skated up.

"Who's going to . . . ?"

"Not me!" said Goldy. "Jude and Danny can fight it out. I don't want to take it."

The bold young Frenchman took it. When the puck was dropped at center ice, the capacity crowd was standing and roaring. Drouin picked it up and started his dash toward the lonely, hulking giant in the Montreal goal. It was David and Goliath all over again. This time Goliath won. Drouin made a fake that caused Dryden to make his move, but Jude held the puck. With an open net in front of him, he shot wide.

The floodgates opened late in the game as the Canadiens swarmed all over their former star goalie, Gump Worsley, who Minnesota had coaxed out of retirement. The North Stars were humbled by a score of 7-2.

In the Minnesota locker room, first-year coach Jack Gordon was talking to his players quietly, as he had done all season. They were not out of it yet. They could come back. Play your position and skate, skate, skate. Don't worry about what your linemate is doing. Play your position and things will begin to break.

When the puck was dropped to start the second game at Montreal, the North Stars did not swoon as anticipated. The flood that Montreal had set loose in the opener went unabated in the first period of the second game, but this time it was the guys in the green, gold and white who were riding the crest.

J.P. Parise, that muscular, hard-digging Frenchman whom the North Stars had given up five players to get out of the Toronto system, scored Minnesota's first goal on a shot that hit goalie Dryden's pads and dribbled in.

Only minutes later, Drouin broke free on a dash down the boards, cut in toward Dryden, and settled an account by snapping a shot through his pads. The pygmies were at the throat of the giant killers.

Still later, while the Canadiens' bad man, John Ferguson, was off for elbowing Goldy, the unrelenting Stars converted again with Ted Hampson scoring on a deflection.

Fate definitely was with the Stars this night. With less than a minute to play in the first period, Murray Oliver swept into the Canadien zone and passed to Lou Nanne on the right side. Nanne fired on goal, Dryden kicked it out, but the rebound was inadvertently tipped in by Mark Tardif, who had predicted a sweep in four games.

The Canadiens came back with strong pressure on goalie Cesare Maniago in the second period, and moved to within striking distance at 4-2. But the Stars' Oliver converted late in the period to make it 5-2.

In the third period, as they had done two nights earlier, The Habs buzzed the Stars' goal tirelessly, firing seventeen shots at Maniago, but only one of them got past the rangy Italian. The Canadiens pulled Dryden in the final minutes and made a six-man rush. But Charlie Burns, as he had done so often throughout the season, broke up the play and led a charge in the other direction toward that unprotected goal. As though to emphasize that fate was on the Stars' side that night, Burns lifted the puck toward the goal and was off target, but it deflected off the Canadiens' Yvan Cournoyer and into the goal.

The final score was Minnesota 6, Montreal 3.

It was a victory for expansion hockey, the first of two that series.

Montreal won the third game by the identical score of 6-3, on the Stars' ice, with Goldy, Grant and Oliver scoring for Minnesota. Perhaps the Minnesota win had been a fluke, since the Canadiens' superior skating and passing was clearly evident in this third game.

Once again the Stars charged back. In the fourth game they were actually skating with the Canadiens, which few teams do. Some teams will check better and play defense better and shoot better, but it is rare that a team will skate better.

For two periods they matched stride for stride and goal for goal, so that at the start of the third the score was 2-2. Something electrifying happened then. A small cluster of the throng of more than 15,000 Stars' fans began a chant to spur their heroes on. The chant spread throughout the jammed arena, so that it became as one boisterous, eerie noise that rattled from wall to wall, deafening, motivating.

As if lifted by the torrent, the Stars flew into the Montreal zone. Bobby Rousseau, another who, like Drouin and Grant, had been dispensible to the Canadiens, fired a shot off Dryden's pads, and the missile bounded to Parise who slapped it home for a 3-2 lead. Still the chant continued. Oliver, who had scored one of the Stars' first two goals, skated in for another, to put Minnesota up 4-2. The success fed the thirst of the spectators, who roared on. Ted Hampson drilled the Stars' fifth and final goal past Dryden.

Montreal was not unaffected by the crowd. Throughout the third the Canadiens fired shot after shot at Maniago, who turned away 15 straight efforts then, and a total of 35 for the game. The final was 5-2, North Stars.

The series was tied at two games each.

When they went back to Montreal there was not a pygmie or giant killer in sight. Just two hockey teams that, if they were not precisely equal, were not that way because of two or three Montreal players. There were the stately Jean Beliveau who, if his skates had lost some of their zip, was still the firm, experienced hand on the controls in a pressure situation, and Frank Mahovlich, the big, rugged winger who had attained superstar status at Toronto before playing at Detroit on the same line as the great Howe. Only a stride away from these two, in greatness, were Henri Richard, who long had lived in the shadow of his older brother, the almost legendary Maurice Richard, who they called the "Rocket," and Yvan Cournoyer, who skated as though he had 707s on each blade.

Again the Stars matched the Canadiens stride for stride through two periods of the fifth game, but were trailing 2-1 when they wilted. Montreal, coming at them as they had through the entire series, always coming, unloaded 19 shots at Maniago in the third, four of them getting by him. It ended 6-1 for the Canadiens to set the stage for the dramatic sixth game.

A packed house at the Met greeted the Stars wildly as they skated out for the final game of that

1970-71 season. At 9:50 of the first period the capacity crowd saw what they had come to see. Defenseman Ted Harris started a rush with Murray Oliver and Charlie Burns, and the fleet Burns rapped home the first goal of the game.

The lead did not stand long. When Danny Grant went off for tripping, Cournoyer scored on a power play.

Early in the second period, Claude LaRose, who had worn the green, gold and white of the North Stars only a year earlier, put Montreal ahead 2-1 after the Stars had failed to clear the puck.

Again defenseman Reid led a rush into the Canadiens' zone, and his rebound was snapped past Dryden by Jude Drouin. It was 2-2.

Both teams were a man short when Montreal's Rejean Houle scored the winning goal at 13:29 of the second period.

When the final rush of that dramatic third period had been made, and the tardy puck lay in the nets behind Dryden, the young goalie looked up in anxiety.

"All I knew was that the puck was in the net, and that my teammates were rushing toward me. I wasn't sure if they were going to hug me or hit me."

After the Stars finally accepted the bitter verdict, they skated to mid-ice and lined up in single file for the ancient Stanley Cup ritual of congratulating each rival player. And then they skated off as they had come on, heads up.

"I'm disappointed by the way it ended," said

Gordon, "but I'm proud at the way we went down. This was a great effort against a great team."

A Montreal columnist wrote:

"The Canadiens discovered the difference between upsetting the Bruins and staving off the unpretentious North Stars. Where they were jubilant over knocking off Boston, they were mostly relieved at getting past the North Stars."

Montreal general manager Sam Pollock, in a moment of generosity (or was it?) said, "The Stars gave us a tougher test than the fabled Boston Bruins."

When all the nice things had been said, the results were still the same: the North Stars were closing down shop for the year while the Canadiens were going to get the Cup.

Goldy had not had a particularly good playoff series, having missed most of the St. Louis set because of the injury and being a trifle out of condition for Montreal as a result. But he was there near the goal mouth when the disputed score hit the nets, and the ending was a bitter pill:

"I guess I got a little upset and charged the referee. I thought for sure it would count, and that meant overtime for us. It was a decisive moment for us because we don't get a chance for a seventh game, and I don't care where you play that seventh game — you can play it on the Nile in Egypt — it's anyone's game.

"We went into this thing confident that we could play with Montreal because we had a pretty good regular season against them. We knew in a series of seven we'd have a good chance. I really think if we would have had Mohns we would have won the series. He gives us a lot of strength on the power play, and he's an old pro. No, he's a young pro by the way he skates. But he's got the knack to carry the puck, to keep possession in their zone. He's got a good shot and he's smart. He helps you back on the blue line, too, because he's got that experience and he always lugs the puck out of our own zone. That is where your game is won or lost, right in your own zone."

While the season had been a fraction too short in the playoffs, there were times during the regular schedule when it may have seemed an endless nightmare to the North Star loyals. At mid-season Minnesota was foundering from its traditional December slump, and Goldy was having his worst scoring year in four with the Stars.

Had it not been for the successes of the franchise in the early years, and the fact that the Stars had been fortified, through trades, with some exciting new players, the home town people might have stayed away from the Met in big bunches. The Stars were miserable at home. They would have one of the worst home records of any club in the league that season.

They had more talent than in any previous year, but putting it all together into a winning combination proved to be a frustrating experience for first year coach Jack Gordon.

Gordon had been to the big time before — but never as a coach. A native of Winnipeg, he had hockey blood in his veins most of his life, and in the 1948-49 season was called out of the minor leagues to

play 31 games with the New York Rangers. He did
not stay there long, playing only one big league game
in the 1949-50 season and four more in 1950-51. Then
he went to Cleveland of the American Hockey
League, and he stayed. For 17 of the 21 years
preceding his arrival in Minnesota, he had either
played with, coached or managed Cleveland. Four
were spent as assistant general manager of the
Rangers.

In his 11 years as Cleveland coach or manager, his
teams won four championships.

Gordon looked at hockey as a general pondering
the troop movements in a war zone: if each unit
moved with precision and carried out its assigned
duties, no matter how independent these movements
appeared, the end result would be a coordinated
campaign that would get the job done.

For some it was a difficult system to adjust to,
because it demanded discipline. Goldy had only
recently become acquainted with discipline.

Right from the start of training camp in that
fourth year Gordon began selling his system, and in
his quiet but firm way he said they either played it his
way or they didn't play at all.

"Goldy, you're a right winger and you take care
of the right side. You don't watch what Grant is
doing on the left side and you don't watch what your
center is doing. You stay on your own side and take
care of that."

That this style of rigid positional hockey did begin
to click late in the season was due, in no small way, to
the caliber of playing personnel the Stars had ac-

cumulated. The talent assembled by Blair, working on the system installed by Gordon, was a refreshing change for the North Star partisans.

For three years they had agonized with their heroes through the ups and downs of an inconsistent team that, most of the time, seemed to have no style of play. They could be positively brilliant one night and absolutely crummy the next. If they had a style, it could best be described as a studied free-for-all.

The draft system had forced them to play major league hockey with untried youths, marginal players, a lot of minor leaguers who would never have had a shot at the big time without expansion, and a sprinkling of those who did have the talent to make it to the top.

Given this type of personnel, the successes they had enjoyed were wrought of raw desire, this injected by the volatile Wren Blair.

If they flooded one side of the rink in their eager pursuit of the elusive puck, and the opposition sprung a man loose over on the other side, the Stars would just have to work that much harder to make up for it. There were advantages to their· helter-skelter style: disorganization breeds disorganization. If the opposition started to play the Stars' brand of hockey, they, the opposition, were dead. Few teams could match Minnesota's superior disorganization.

At times their play resulted in sheer terror for their own goaltenders, because when they were on the attack they might make a challenge on the point while everyone else was deep in the opponent's zone, and this would result in a three-man breakaway for the other guys. Goalies do not like three-man breakaways unless the trio is wearing their kind of jersey and heading in the other direction.

Most of this would change in season number four, but not immediately. There was still the matter of timing to be developed between players who had not skated together before. But given the talent, that would come.

Jack Gordon was a coach who operated like a businessman. He believed in management by objectives. You determine a specific goal or objective for the year, and develop the strategy for achieving it. His primary objective was to cut down the Stars' goals-against record. They had given up 257 goals in the previous season, the second worst figure in the entire NHL.

"He told us," said Goldy, "that if we set objectives, then we would bear down to meet them, and in the process we would win games. He set our objective of goals-against at 215, and we ended the season with 221."

There were problems for Jack Gordon that year. For one thing, Tommy Williams had suffered that back injury in training, and this meant the breaking up of the Goldy-Williams-Parise line. Goldy, and consequently the entire team, would suffer mightily as a result, at least through the first half of the 1970-71 season.

Gordon had also come into a situation where the previous year's coach was now expected to play and produce for him, an awkward situation, at best. That this proved to be more of an advantage than a handicap to the new bench boss was due primarily to the nature of the man he succeeded. Charlie Burns did not hang his head and pout. Every time he took the ice for Gordon he was like a buzz saw, skating, skating, skating, breaking up the opposition's power play before it could get organized, doing whatever he was asked to do and giving 110 per cent all the time.

"Charlie had been coach and I thought it would be a ticklish deal," said Gordon, "but instead the guy simply went out of his way to help in a hundred ways, while giving everything he had on the ice. The players developed great respect for Charlie, and that's so important to a team's discipline."

Through the first half of that fourth season the North Stars' management was not pleased with the play of its team, and the greatest disappointment was Goldy.

Wren Blair summoned the big winger to his office near mid-season, and as he had done so many times before — with Goldy and other players he knew were not playing to their potential — probed for a way to ignite him.

"I'll tell you what's the matter with you," said Blair, "you're overweight and your head is as big as a pumpkin because you had one good season. You think one season makes a career?"

Both Blair and his new coach, sharing a common faith in Goldy, worked at trying to get him untracked. But it did not happen until after the All-Star game break. A year earlier, Goldy had 18 goals and had been chosen to compete in that showing of the NHL's elite. Now he had but six goals, and Tommy Williams, whom he had counted on to pull him out of his scoring slump, would shortly be on the way to Oakland.

Then Goldy was put on the line with Grant on the left side and the rookie Drouin between them, and the Goldy shuffle came back into style once more in Minnesota.

The North Stars also began to jell in late season, playing a more conservative style of hockey than previously. If they were playing poorly on offense, Gordon would have only one man forechecking and the rest dropping back in a tight defensive pattern. When the offense was moving, he would have two men forechecking and only one dropping back with the defense.

At team meetings the day of a game, Gordon would go over each of the opposing players with the individuals who would be playing against them, with a few words of advice.

"J. P., you're going to be covering Cournoyer tonight. Just be a little aware of him."

That meant Parise wasn't to give up his offensive charges down the boards, but that he should be slightly more defensive minded than usual. He should not commit himself as much as if he were playing against someone else, or the jet-bladed Cournoyer would be a blur streaking off on a breakaway.

Even with their new system and the addition of some fine new players, the Stars were not a smashing success through the regular season, going down to the final moments of the campaign to win a playoff spot with a fourth place finish.

When the Stanley Cup playoffs started, the Stars were counting heavily on the streaking Goldsworthy to help them break the hex St. Louis seemed to have on them. Twice before the two expansion teams had met in the Western Division playoffs, and in each instance the Blues had ousted the Stars in rough and tumble series. And this time the Blues were coming off a late season hot streak, while the Stars had a four-game losing streak.

St. Louis, unlike the North Stars, had not gone primarily for youth in the expansion draft. The Blues picked up a number of tough veteran players that gave them an initial edge over the other expansion teams. And they had built an image of being a gang of bullies who always tried to intimidate the opposition.

"We knew they would come out and try to intimidate us again, just like in the previous series," said Goldy. "We had that old rivalry going for some reason. I don't think they have much love for us and we don't for them."

The first game was played in St. Louis, a city that's image was once built around brewery horses and Stan Musial, a gentle, kindly man who used to rip the seams out of baseballs for the Cardinals. St. Louis hockey fans may not remember Stan Musial, and they have little time for brewery horses unless they are pulling their assigned cargo. They are a raucous, screaming mob given to littering the ice over the least little displeasure inflicted upon them, or even attacking visiting players. Once, in the first game of that series in the spring of 1971, a fan threw a cup of beer on Goldy's head as he was going out after the period. The moisture would not help fill out Goldy's thinning crop of hair, according to his close friend Parise, "because you can't grow grass on a rock."

Goldy went after the fan, and the ever-present police broke up the ensuing melee.

The conduct of the fans was infectious, or perhaps it was the conduct of the Blues that infected the fans. In either case, the Blues opened the series as though they were competing for the tag-team wrestling championship rather than something so stately as Lord Stanley's silver cup. They knew they could not skate with the North Stars, much less with someone like the Montreal Canadiens or the Boston Bruins. They would have to win with brute strength, not finesse. If the champagne were to flow in the Blues' dressing room, a little blood must first be let on the ice.

The first period of game one was like an Irish tavern scene on St. Patrick's Day. St. Louis took shot after shot at Goldy, Danny Grant and defenseman Ted Harris, and the door to the penalty box was swinging open and shut like a revolving door. At one time, each team had only three skaters on the ice, and St. Louis was intent on trying to flatten those three remaining North Stars. Then they'd have only the goalie to beat.

Minnesota did not come to brawl, but the Stars did come prepared to make a stand. This time they would not be intimidated. Their own defensemen, big Ted Harris who came over from Montreal with a reputation as a good fighter, and Tom Reid and

Barry Gibbs, who could handle themselves well when the sticks and gloves were thrown aside for more serious business, would see to it that the Stars did not back down against the St. Louis challenge.

When the Blues finally decided they were not going to chase the Stars off the ice, they played a superior brand of hockey, firing 44 shots — twice the number of the Stars — at Cesare Maniago. But the tall goalie was sensational, and Minnesota scored on two third-period power play goals by Parise and Grant to win 3-2.

It was a stunning loss for the Blues, even though they did accomplish one of their objectives. They took Goldy out of action on Plager's vicious, low check late in the game. The man the Stars had felt indispensible to victory over the Blues would be on crutches when Minnesota celebrated its conquest of St. Louis.

Coach Gordon was downcast over the loss of Goldy. "He is one of our two or three key players. He is particularly important on the power play. Now I look down the bench and really don't know what I am going to do. Goldy is a heck of a guy to put on the ice with about 40 seconds left killing penalties because he controls the play so well."

Later, when the series was over and someone had marvelled at the fact the Stars won in spite of Goldy's absence, a local columnist speculated that it might have happened because Goldy was out. "Instead of relying too much on Goldy the Stars had to improvise. They learned they were better hockey players than they thought they were. If they remember this when Goldy returns, if they continue to play a versatile game, all trusting one another, they will be a better team and Goldy will become an even better hockey player."

That the champagne did flow in the Twin Cities and not St. Louis, despite the absence of Goldy, was attributed in large measure to three gentlemen who heretofore had played solid but unspectacular hockey. Gordon, in an effort to put together a checking line to ride herd on St. Louis' top scoring line, put Murray Oliver at Center between Charlie Burns and Lou Nanne.

Oliver had come over from Toronto with a reputation as a steady, consistent player who usually accumulated about fifty points a season and who was an excellent penalty killer.

Burns was a veteran who could skate all day and could play any position, though he had been used mostly to kill penalties.

Nanne, when he was used, had also played mostly on defense. That he played at all seemed a mystery to some hockey people, because Nanne makes the game look like a herculean effort every time he hits the ice. He skates with powerful outward strides like a skier walking up hill. But he works and sweats like he were playing in a sauna and bulls his way along the boards with fearless determination, to the great delight of the Minnesota partisans.

It was these three, who had been put together to stop the St. Louis attack, that provided the Stars their much needed scoring punch when Goldy departed.

"We knew we had to dig a little deeper to take up

the slack caused by Goldy's loss," said Oliver. "Goldy's line carried us into the playoffs. He was our cannon. Without him, we all had to bear down a little harder."

Oliver bore down, getting two goals in the second game at St. Louis, but it was not enough, as the Blues belted out a 4-2 win to even things at one game each.

The absence of Goldy's scoring punch began to look like the demise of the Stars in the third game, this one in Minnesota, when St. Louis skated to a 3-0 victory and a two game to one lead in the series.

Furthermore, the punchless Stars were shut out for two more periods in the fourth game, and went into the third trailing 1-0. Spurred by another of those thunderous crowd efforts, the Stars finally broke their scoring drought with a goal by Bobby Rousseau, to tie it at 1-1. Then, Charlie Burns, who escaped serious injury when he was checked into a penalty box door that had accidentally come open, scored the winner on a brilliant play. Defenseman Doug Mohns had carried the puck out of his own zone, and hit Oliver with a perfect pass. Oliver dumped it to the waddling Nanne, who got it to Burns for the score.

The series was tied at two games each.

It was back to St. Louis to once again face that jeering, heckling mob.

Before leaving for the St. Louis arena, Nanne, who skates with all the grace of a fast-walking duck, said he hoped it would be his last game.

"Before every game I say I hope it's my last. It's the pressure that makes me feel this way. But five minutes after the start, everything is different. If we win, I say I want to play until I'm forty. If we lose, then I want to play again to rectify any mistakes."

Nanne had no mistakes to rectify in this fifth game. With less than four minutes to play in a rough contest that was tied at 3-3, Nanne scored the biggest goal of his short career to give the Stars a victory and a three to two game lead in the series.

Minnesota went home to beat the Blues, 5-2, with a burst of four goals late in the second period. It was the first time St. Louis had suffered a playoff series loss to another expansion club. One of the heroes of that last game was 37-year-old veteran defenseman Dough Mohns, who scored two goals. But as their hopes faded, the Blues played on as they had all season, bruising, punishing, bullying the opposition, and one of those low checks by Bob Plager caught Mohns across the knees.

Mohns would not return for the climactic showdown with Montreal.

The North Stars would finish their season one second and one man short.

Chapter XIII

A Quarter Inch to Darkness

Wren Blair turned to his assistant general manager, John Mariucci, and said, "John, will you tell the stewardess not to serve our players? We'll have steaks somewhere when we get to Philadelphia."

The Stars were enroute to Philadelphia by a charter flight they were sharing with the Philadelphia 76ers basketball team.

Mariucci walked up to the stewardess and said, "Please don't serve our hockey players; we'll eat when we get there."

"How do I know which ones are your players?" asked the young lady.

Looking back over the mixture of hockey and basketball players, Mariucci said: "Mine are the short, white ones."

Hockey is a funny, violent, dangerous game, surrounded by superstitions and rituals.

For the Minnesota North Stars the humor has been provided by people like Mariucci, who came out of Minnesota's Iron Range to play five years with the Chicago Black Hawks in the 1940s; Gump

Worsley, that ancient goalie who does not look like he is having fun when he is in the nets; and by others such as defenseman Tom Reid, a prankster, and Danny Grant, who deals in dry humor.

Grant's humor is as quick as his blazing shot, and after his wife gave birth to their first child, a girl, Grant said:

"I'm glad it's a girl. Now I won't have to worry about her becoming a hockey player."

"But you'll have to worry about her getting mixed up with a hockey player," said Goldy.

"Then I hope it's one like Jude, not like you," Grant shot back.

A favorite prank between Goldy and J.P. Parise, often roommates on road trips, was to turn up the heat in the other's electric blanket, until one night Goldy devised a scheme that ended that business. He switched cords to the two electric blankets before J.P. came in. When they went to bed, J.P. reached over and turned Goldy's dial to high. Later that night, Parise thought he was coming down with a fever when he started to sweat under his red-hot blanket.

Gump Worsley has long been considered one of the funny men in the NHL, and this may have been due to the constant danger he lived with while on the ice. Every time Gump or his stablemate, Cesare Maniago, went on the ice, people would be shooting a piece of brick-like rubber at them, sometimes at speeds of 100 miles an hour. (They and the other goalies in the league had one thought in common that went through their minds whenever they played the Chicago Black Hawks: "Oh, God, Hull's got the puck!")

Cesare did what almost every other goalie did, he got himself a plastic face mask. Gump, who had started blocking flying pucks about the time Washington was pitching silver dollars over the Delaware, could not change his habits when the face mask came into vogue.

Asked once why he was one of the few goalies around who was not wearing a mask, Gump replied: "What do you mean? I'm wearing one now."

"If Gump got hit in the face by a puck, it could only improve his looks," said Mariucci, whose own face resembles a heavily-used practice rink that had begun to melt.

"If that's the case," said Gump, "then you'd have to get hit in the face by a bus."

In a training camp interview before the Stars' fourth season, Maniago reported that "Gump has lost one and a half pounds, and is in great shape. He's done two knee bends and one and a half pushups."

Asked how much he weighed, Gump replied: "About 180 pounds."

"Is that firm?" asked the interviewer.

"No," said Gump. "I never look at the scales."

Gump was never fond of flying, and his feeling of uneasiness was not helped by a flight he was on once with the Montreal Canadiens. The jet had hit an air pocket and dropped about 2,000 feet, and the food the team was being served at the time flew all over their clothing. The captain emerged from the cabin and said, "We're sorry about the turbulence, it came on rather unexpectedly. The airline will take care of the dry cleaning of your suits."

Gump stood up and said, "What about our shorts?"

Humor is hockey's pressure valve, because it is a game of severe tension that often spawns violence.

That Goldy became involved in many slugfests over the years was due, in part, to the intensity of the pressure that he would feel every day he was to play.

"On those days, I'm total concentration on the game," he said. "I keep thinking about all the left wings and left defensemen I might play against, and I get so nervous that my hands sweat. Even at the start of the game I have to spray my hands to make them sticky.

"You get so keyed up sometimes, and then if things aren't going well for you it doesn't take much for you to blow up. Some nights you try so hard and nothing is going right, and you know it's one of those bad situations where you have to do something. So some guy takes a run at you, and that's it."

Game days have always been hard on June. After suffering through a morning of Goldy's brooding silence, she makes him a steak and salad at 1 p.m. He won't eat again until late that night, after the game.

June and Tammy sit down with Goldy at lunch, and she tries to carry on a conversation, but usually to no avail.

"Please say something, anything!" she says in frustration. He says little. His mind is several hours in the future, focused on all those guys he must try to beat that night.

Some hockey people say talk about violence in the game is exaggerated.

"Even when they get in a fight, it's not that violent," Wren Blair contends, "because it's spontaneous. It lasts maybe ten seconds and no one can throw a good punch while on skates, anyway. Besides, what's wrong with a good fight? I always thought Americans were people who like to fight. Everybody loves a fight. In Canada we always figured we could settle things quicker with a good fight than screwing around with an argument for four days, or by staying mad for four years."

Even so, NHL President Campbell has started to get tough about fighting by issuing more severe fines. Goldy is among those he has issued strongly-worded warnings to.

"I know that if I have one more big run-in with him," said Goldy, "I'll probably be sitting out awhile. He's told me that. I can't go wild out there now because it's going to cost me money you wouldn't believe."

Violence aside, injuries suffered in the course of action remain the greatest threat to a hockey player's career.

It could have ended at one of several times for Goldy, and there might never have been that 36-goal season in which he beat out the great Howe and all the other right wingers in the NHL, or had that amazing streak of 28 goals over 28 games.

The hazards he lived with were certainly no greater than those of hundreds of other professional athletes, and probably a lot less than those for people who make their living travelling the dangerous highways. But Goldy had always played hockey in a manner that it seemed hazardous to him personally, and several times along the way his career had been threatened by injuries.

He had received a proper share of stitches over the years — perhaps more than his share — because when the fists started flying he always seemed to be in the middle of the melee. But stitches were a routine thing. Once he had his tongue split open. This required ten stitches to close.

There was a day in Chicago Goldy would not forget. It was during that big third season when the Stars' right winger scored 36 goals. Goldy and Tommy Williams had a partial break, with only the Hawks' Pit Martin to beat. Goldy rushed in with the puck and tried to get around Martin. As he used his body to protect the puck, Martin made a move to poke check him. The stick came up and hit the Stars' winger across the bridge of the nose and along the eyelid. He knew he had been cut, but the gash didn't start to bleed right away.

After a brief examination of the wound at the bench, Goldy was sent to the dressing room. The club doctor from Chicago worked for a long time, putting twenty stitches in the long wound. By the time he was finished, the eye was swollen shut.

Then he stood back and looked at Goldy.

"If that had been a quarter of an inch deeper, you could have lost that eye," said the doctor.

Goldy was not concerned at the time, because he hadn't looked at the eye, but later when he did, he realized how bad it was.

June had listened to the game on the radio and heard he had been cut, but didn't know it was the eye. She was shocked when he came home the next day, because it was not the ordinary kind of cut and one side of his face was badly swollen.

"I got quite concerned," said Goldy, "because I was wondering if there was going to be any false vision or double vision, since a blow like that can affect the pupil by causing hemorrhaging. As it turned out, I was quite fortunate. There has been no change in my vision. I still can't see."

Goldy had never been seriously injured in hockey as a child or through the days of Junior A competition, but for the occasional loss of a tooth, and that is of little import. Hockey was invented by the tooth fairy.

Professional hockey was different, because everyone was playing for money and glory, and it was a hard, bruising, punishing style of play where one check that caught a man off balance could take him off the ice for a week, a month, a season, perhaps a career.

Goldy's reckless, driving, thumping style of play would get him a damaging blow now and again. One of these would become the subject of some discussion over the merits of hockey helmets.

In a game just before the All-Star break of that 1970-71 season, when Goldy was still in the throes of that scoring slump, Buffalo had come to play at the Met. The Sabres had a trouble-making dynamo named Eddie Shack, who raced hither and yon over the ice delivering bumps and bruises in a perfectly indiscriminate way, so that it did not take long before a lot of people on the opposing team were mad at him. Sometimes they got back at him. Sometimes not.

Shack had picked up a loose puck and was approximately equidistant from the two sides of the rink when both Goldy and his opposite wing, J.P. Parise, who is built like a mini-semi truck and is rated at about the same horsepower, went after him. Both later denied any evil intent, though under Jack Gordon's system neither was supposed to be that far out away from the boards. When they arrived at what had been the location of Shack, he was not there. They collided. Goldy fell to the ice, his ear slashed open, and it was several minutes before he knew where he was.

"If you want to play again, I think you should consider wearing a helmet," the doctor said later, after conducting some tests.

Goldy put on a helmet for the first time in his career. And then he went out and played that big second half when he scored 28 goals in 28 games. Many people debated whether it was coincidence or not — the helmet and the scoring spree.

One who did not debate the issue was J.P., who had met Goldy at mid-ice on that unfortunate occasion. His answer, when asked what the difference had been in Goldy's style of play during the slump and after, was a blunt "No difference."

The blackout was not the first Goldy had experienced in the professional ranks. Twice before, at Oklahoma City and Boston, he had been blind-sided into the boards and knocked unconscious.

"When it happens," he said, "it always happens that way. They come at you from the blind side and you aren't expecting it. You figure you got one guy beat but it's the other guy coming around behind you, and 'bang,' he hits you.

"A lot of people asked me why I started wearing the helmet when I hadn't before. It's a tough question to answer. I don't think I really took into account what I had at stake until I had two close calls. Then I said, 'Well, that's two, and you can never tell about the next one, maybe it's the final one.' I figured why take a chance? A lot of players haven't experienced anything like that, like coming within a quarter of an inch of losing an eye or getting knocked out, so they don't have the attitude for wearing a helmet.

"I started taking account of myself and I figured the helmet was like insurance. It could extend my career, because when I go out on the ice I don't let up. That's the way I play."

The controversy over hockey helmets will not be resolved soon. There are heated arguments on both sides. Bill Masterton, who had been on the same line with Goldy that night in 1968 when he fell and struck his head on the ice, only to die several days later, was not wearing a helmet.

Wren Blair is adamant over the subject of helmets.

"I say helmets are optional. If they want to wear them, they do. You never hear that question in Canada. I'll tell you one thing, if you're talking about safety and worrying about people dying, if you don't let kids drive cars until they're 18 you'll save more lives by the noon hour that first day than you'll save in the entire history of hockey if helmets had been used.

"One thing I'm against is mandatory use of helmets. This is a democracy and these guys are pros. They should have the right to decide. If a guy wants to be a stock car racer, you may say, 'Ya, but guys get killed driving stock cars,' but just the same that's up to him. He has a right to choose.

"Selfishly, the thing I don't like about helmets is the showmanship angle. With helmets they all look like robots out there. People bring up pro football to counter this, but in football you're nine miles from the game anyway. In hockey a player is right here in front of you. If a guy is a redhead or a blonde, you identify with him. So maybe they get belted around a little, that's why they get big money. Still, it is and always has been up to a player himself whether or not he wears a helmet. We neither encourage or discourage it. A lot of players who have tried helmets for a time have quit wearing them, and either way it's fine with me. I just don't think anyone has a right to dictate to major league players that they have to wear head gear.

"The minute you say something like this a whole lot of people get uptight, and think that what you're saying is you want your players to get hurt, and that's not it at all. I know people like to see the players and the color of their hair and everything else.

"Certainly Goldy has lost a lot of identity with his helmet on. He's blonde and a lot of people would

identify with him. People who have been coming for
some time will know him, but the new fans will never
totally identify with Goldy as they did before."

A number of North Stars wore helmets in that
1970-71 season, and some who might have benefited
from them most did not.

"If anyone should wear a helmet," said Goldy,
"it's J.P. The way he goes down those boards — he
just bulls his way through."

Charlie Burns has long worn a helmet, because of
a metal plate in his head.

When Goldy was a guest at a father-and-son
banquet following the 1970-71 season, a youngster
asked him: "Do you think the helmet was the reason
you scored all those goals?"

"Heck, no. If I thought that were the case, I'd
wear two helmets."

While helmets will long be the biggest source of
controversy over hockey injuries, spectators are, in
many ways, the greatest threat to causing serious
injury. In their excitement, be it anger or delight,
they impulsively throw things on the ice, some of
which may escape detection.

Metallic things, like paper clips or coins, are a
constant cause of concern, because paper clips are
hard to see and coins will melt the ice and become
imbedded so that the top side is flush with the playing
surface. A player streaking along at twenty to thirty
miles an hour on skates might hit one of these things
and lose control completely. Then he is flying
through the air grabbing at something to hold onto,
with the boards coming at him rapidly, but there is
nothing to grab. The boards do not give.

Such an incident had occurred to a player on the Kitchener-Waterloo Dutchmen when Goldy was a youngster, and he never forgot it because the player involved did not play hockey again.

"The Dutchmen were playing Sudbury," Goldy recalled, "and this guy named Jack McMasters was coming down the ice fast when he hit a paper clip or a piece of paper and lost control. He was considered one of the best prospects Toronto ever had. But he was hurt badly in that game and was crippled from the waist down. After that he had to use canes to walk."

In their agitation over the course of events, fans will throw almost anything on the ice: beer cans, pop cans, programs, ice cream, firecrackers, money — anything within reach.

In a game against St. Louis Goldy had scored the hat trick, and as he skated back for the faceoff, an upper plate of false teeth came skidding across the ice at him.

"It was a whole upper plate. I couldn't believe it. This guy apparently was so happy he just took out the plate and threw it, and it skidded across the ice and hit my skate blade. If the plate would have fit I might have kept it, but instead I took if over to the penalty box. It wasn't one of those fake plates, either."

In another game when Goldy had scored the go-ahead goal, a woman threw her brassiere on the ice. Like a gentleman, Goldy skated over, speared it with his stick, and took it over to the timekeeper's table.

Some fans obviously come to a game with the intention of throwing something on the ice. When the Stars were playing at Chicago an octopus was tossed out. The Stars could have used such a creature in goal during their early years, with a glove on each of its eight arms.

At the Met one night a bag with a duck and pheasant in it came sailing over the boards. They were still alive, and the players and officials milled around, not knowing how to handle the situation. St. Louis' star forward, Red Berenson, an outdoor sportsman type of fellow, came to their rescue and got the birds off the ice.

Spectators get so wrapped up in a game that occasionally they will act without reason or restraint. The Stars were playing poorly and getting beat in a game at Met Sports Center when they got the power play advantage.

Goldy was carrying the puck up the ice and some fan was either mad at him or the way the game was going, because he stopped an ice cream vendor, bought a whole box of those little ice cream cups, went up to the glass and tossed the entire thing over. Goldy was trying to carry the puck and weave his way through all those cups. Finally, in disgust, he shot the puck over the boards.

Refuse thrown on the ice always stops play, and frequently it stops the momentum of a team. The delay can cool off a team that is hot, or give a much-needed break in the action for one that is having difficulties.

Despite the conduct of the spectators, the bruising, body-checking style of play that has always typified Canadian hockey, is the source of the vast majority of injuries. Goldy was by no means injury prone, but both he and the North Stars suffered some damage over those first four years.

Prior to being kayoed by J.P. in the collision that led to putting on the helmet, Goldy had several brushes with potentially serious injuries. In a game at Minnesota he had been checked into the goal post and fell heavily to the ice. He lay there motionless, blood spurting from his arm. The first announcement was that he had suffered a broken forearm and sustained severe bruises and lacerations. But when all the blood had been washed away and the X-rays taken, it proved to be only a deep cut on the arm all the way down to the bone. The impact upon hitting the goal had been so great that the arm had just split open. The doctors snipped the veins together and sewed up the gash.

The shot to the knee he took from Bob Plager in the 1971 Cup playoffs aggravated the previous injury in Oklahoma when he had gone under the knife twice, but fortunately there was little cartilage left in the knee to be damaged.

The North Stars suffered two other key injuries that season: one was the loss of Doug Mohns in the playoffs and the other the mishap to defenseman Fred Barrett. Barrett was going full steam when he crashed into the goal post in a game against Detroit. He suffered a broken thigh bone, a rare hockey injury that sidelined him for the remainder of that season.

Minnesota also lost the services of Gump for a time during 1971, when he pulled a groin muscle.

While Goldy's career had been in jeopardy due to injuries, the man he had idolized as a child back in Kitchener, very nearly had his life, as well as his career, wiped out by a hockey injury.

It was 1950, and Gordy Howe was playing his third season with the Detroit Red Wings. In a Stanley Cup playoff game Howe collided with Toronto's Ted Kennedy, then crashed head-on into the sideboards.

Howe was rushed to a hospital. He had suffered a severe brain injury. The man who the hockey world would later come to regard as indestructible, lingered at the edge of death for several days while surgeons operated to relieve pressure on his brain.

Thereafter, Gordy Howe had a slight facial tic that, at times, caused his dark eyes to blink uncontrollably. He became known to his teammates as "Blinky," but he was too big a man to let this bother him.

Chapter XIV

Thirst for the Cup

Bobby Hull raises prize bulls. Some people say he wrestles them. It's possible he may have wrestled them to get into condition for the NHL expansion season of 1967-68, because the powerful blonde forward of the Chicago Black Hawks went out and set an NHL record that season with 54 goals. Quite possibly the caliber of the competition that year helped him to the record. In his previous four years with the Hawks, Bobby had seasons of 13, 18, 39 and 31 goals.

Phil Esposito does not raise bulls — he plays on a whole team of them. And while Esposito has been derided in some quarters for scoring a lot of "garbage" goals, he erased Hull's one-season record with an amazing total of 76 goals in the fourth year of expansion hockey.

So, when the North Stars and their five cousins in the West took to the ice that first season, these were the kinds of guys the East had, the superstars who gave the established teams that one or two goal advantage in every meeting between the two divisions.

211

"Every time we played one of those East teams, we knew we were in for a tough game," said Goldy. "But we had considerable pride. Take a game against Boston — some of our guys, including myself, wanted to show them they made a mistake in letting us go in the draft, so we were out there to give it all we had. When we played Montreal, guys like Danny Grant and Claude LaRose wanted to show them they were wrong, too.

"But they had the Hull's and the Esposito's and guys like Gordy Howe and Mahovlich and Beliveau, and that made it tough on us. I'll tell you something, I wouldn't wrestle one of Bobby Hull's bulls, and what's more, I wouldn't wrestle Bobby Hull. That guy is amazing. He's smart, strong and has that fantastic shot. You know, you don't see him get into many fights, because when he does, he never loses."

It was always an interesting experience for Goldy when the North Stars went into Chicago for a game against the Black Hawks. There would be the usual team meeting in the coach's suite the afternoon before the game, and Jack Gordon would go over the Hawks' roster with his players.

"Tonight we'll pair off this way," said Gordon. "Jude, we want you to play against Chico Maki and Dennis Hull, or whoever they have on the right side. Goldy, that means you have to watch Bobby."

"Thanks, Jack, thank you very much."

"He wears the same kind of pants you do," said Gordon, trying to build the confidence of his big wing.

But Goldy never really minded playing against Hull. "I like to play against him because he's a real fine competitor and he respects the fact that he is going to be checked, and that he's always going to have a guy on him. Just the same, it's hard to check him because he roams a lot. He roams to cause confusion. He doesn't play position but he's still got a guy on him all the time. He plays 78 games with someone on his back."

It is not surprising. The people who keep records of such things say that Hull is the fastest skater in the NHL, having been clocked at 29.7 mph without the puck and 28.3 mph with it. Some people don't drive that fast. Hull's slap shot has been clocked at 118.3 mph, which figures out to about 35 mph over the average in the league.

If those statistics were not enough to make the opposition stand in awe of the Black Hawk superstar, his physical dimensions might be. At 5-10 and 195 pounds, he has legs like a fullback, and his upper dimensions — biceps, chest and neck — are greater than any heavyweight boxing champion since Rocky Marciano.

While expansion provided the Eastern players the opportunity to fatten their statistics, and thereby their pocket books, it offered some goalies in the West the opportunity to win medals for bravery. In that first year when the North Stars went east for their first encounter with an established team on its home ice, they were nearly shelled back across the Hudson River by the New York Rangers. The Rangers used their former goalie, Cesare Maniago, for target practice, bombarding him with a record 56 shots. Despite heroic efforts on the part of the tall goaltender, New York won, 5-2. In the third period alone, the Rangers got off 23 shots on goal — about as many as the Stars got in an entire game with the Eastern clubs.

The rallying cry of the North Stars in those days was: "Hey, stop that one, Cese . . . look out, here comes another one, Cese!"

Maniago's body would be covered with large bruises and welts throughout the season.

Even though Gump didn't come over from Montreal until the fourth season, he, too, suffered through some trying times. In a game at Boston he was shelled by 64 shots. When the debacle was over, he told his teammates, "I'm going to sue you guys for non-support."

Through their early years, desire was the only advantage the West took into a contest with the loaded Eastern teams, and if the West did not win too many of those clashes, they did, at least, achieve some measure of success: they survived.

The playoffs were different, because then everything was even in the matter of desire, and the East had all the other advantages. Through the first three years they pummeled the expansion clubs mercilessly. It was all because of the Cup.

Lord Stanley's Cup is an imposing hunk of silver with a Canadian heritage and a reluctance to go south over the border into the United States. The Montreal Canadiens have long considered the Cup their personal trophy, and they have drunk several wine cellars of champagne from it over the years. It has been the history of the National Hockey League that anyone who wants to lay claim to the Cup must first challenge the proud Canadiens, who get so high when the thing is at stake that it would seem they had drunk from it before, not after, their conquest.

Even the Montreal fans get higher than a pot party for the Cup playoffs, so high that once they almost tore down the Forum. The great Rocket Richard, that fiery-tempered leader of the Canadiens for so many years, had been suspended from the playoffs for striking an official. A riot broke out in the Forum, resulting in thousands of dollars of damage and forfeit of the game.

The Cup was contributed to Canadian hockey in 1893 by Lord Stanley of Preston, the Earl of Derby and then Governor-General of Canada. The punch bowl shaped trophy started on a zany career as an award signifying supremacy in Canadian amateur hockey. As if by predestination, a Montreal team won it that first year. Later it wandered over into the National Hockey Association, a forerunner of the NHL.

Purchased originally for a price of $48.67, the Cup has undergone alterations, including the engraving of names on it, that have cost in excess of $14,000. All of this looks like pocket money compared to the colossal sums hockey people have spent trying to win the thing.

In its seventy some years of wandering back and forth across the continent, the Cup has endured many adventures. It was once booted into a canal by its happy possessors, who learned with much relief the following day that the canal was frozen over. Another time it was left in a photographer's studio after it had posed with its winner, and the photographer's mother, not aware of its stately purpose, filled it with dirt and planted geraniums in it.

During a scuffle over possession of the thing one year, between members of the team that had already won it, the much cherished Cup was thrown over a fence into a cemetery.

Montreal's chances of drinking from the Cup in the spring of 1971 were considered as preposterous as the Cup being used for a flower pot. The Canadiens had not had a particularly impressive season, and for the first round of the playoffs they drew the Boston Bruins, who, at one time considered merely impressive, were then considered awesome. Scoring records by the ton had fallen to their advance.

But in hockey the team with the best physical qualifications does not always win. It is a game of passion over proficiency, as Wren Blair had proved by taking his first year North Stars to within one game of the Cup playoff finals.

After stunning the Bruins, the Canadiens beat the Stars in six games and the Chicago Black Hawks in seven, and the wine once again flowed from the great silver chalice in the Montreal Forum.

Whether the North Stars had given the Canadiens a greater test than the mighty Bruins, as one Montreal executive had said, is of doubtful validity and little consequence. That the Stars did, indeed, offer a genuine challenge to the Cup winners may have been the beginning of a new era for the NHL.

It may have taken four years of futility on the part of the expansion teams to begin approaching anything like parity with the established clubs, but the draft system formulated in 1967 was beginning to spread the talent around in a more uniform manner.

To be sure, something was still missing in the ranks of the expansion teams, that only time could cure: experience. That and the superstars. But even superstars must retire some day. The indestructible Howe has finally hung up his skates, to the great relief of many who tried to stop him.

Jean Beliveau retired. Hull is in his 30s, not old for a hockey player, but still near or past the midway point of his brilliant career. Esposito and Frank Mahovlich are also in their 30s.

The mere mortals of the NHL must live with Orr for many more years.

"They should put that guy in a league all by himself," Goldy said once.

The North Stars had, by the end of that 1970-71 season, sprinkled their lineup with experience, even though they had not accomplished this by standing firm with their original draft choices. There was just Goldy and Cesare left. All the others were gone. Some, like Wayne Connelly and Billy Collins and Dave Balon, their first draft choice back in 1967, had become established players in the NHL. But the departure of these was offset by the arrival of other good hockey players — some young, some not so young — who gave the North Stars the blend of youthful vigor and experience with which to make their strong playoff bid in the spring of 1971.

Defense had been one key to their success. In Ted Harris and Doug Mohns they had obtained experience to go with their promising younger defensemen — Barry Gibbs, Tom Reid and Fred Barrett.

Harris had played for Jack Gordon at Cleveland before going up to the big show with Montreal in 1964. There he spent seven blissful seasons knocking down people who dared to insult the proud Canadiens by carrying a puck into their zone. At 6-2 and 180 pounds, not many people tried to argue with him.

More experienced and completely different in style than Harris, Mohns was a rushing defenseman who not only carried the puck deftly out of his own zone but also was a scoring threat. At 37, he had 17 years of NHL experience, eleven at Boston and six at Chicago. In four of his last five seasons with the Black Hawks he had scored over 20 goals. He had a hard, accurate shot, and, like Charlie Burns, could begin skating in the fall and not stop until the ice started to melt.

Gibbs came out of the Bruin organization with a reputation as a tough guy who would take his lumps and his penalties in big doses, and this he had lived up to. With Oklahoma City the year prior to coming to Minnesota he had led the league in penalty minutes with 194. He fell slightly off that pace in the

1969-70 season, his first with the Stars, when he logged only 182 in the penalty box.

The rookie Barrett, who suffered a broken thigh bone in the second half, had come to the Stars right out of Junior A hockey, and had been so impressive at moving and passing the puck in training camp that he had stayed on.

Reid, acquired in the 1968-69 season as part of a four-player swap with the Chicago Black Hawks, could not rush like Mohns or hit like Harris, but had a combination of skills of which dependable defensemen are made.

The green light had barely begun blinking over that one-second-too-late goal in 1971 before The Bird was looking around for someone to deal with, and maybe speed up the arrival of that parity business. Their defense firmed up, the Stars needed more scoring punch, and Blair got Oakland's Dennis Hextall, who had once been in the main event with Goldy on a fight card at a meeting between the Stars and Seals, and Bob Nevin from the New York Rangers.

For Hextall they gave up the promising young Joey Johnston and center Walt McKechnie. Hextall, whose father, Bryan, had played 11 seasons with the New York Rangers and has been enshrined in Hockey's Hall of Fame, had his best year in three in the majors during the 1970-71 compaign, scoring 21 goals and 31 assists. A plucky, hard-nosed competitor, he accumulated 217 minutes in penalties — more than any North Star got that season.

Blair gave up veteran Bobby Rousseau to get Nevin, a 13-year NHL veteran with a career total of more than 200 goals.

The Bird made one other move in the months following the 1971 playoffs, signing Gary Gambucci, who, like the departed Tommy Williams, is a native of Minnesota. Gambucci came out of Hibbing for an impressive collegiate career at the University of Minnesota, and was a standout scorer for the U.S. National team.

The rookie Drouin was the greatest find in that fourth year of the North Stars, and the detractors who had jumped The Bird for giving up the popular Billy Collins soon forgot. The young, brassy French-man, who had won the American Hockey League scoring title with 106 points on 37 goals and 69 assists the previous season with the Montreal Voyageurs, made the loss of the playmaking Tommy Williams less painful. He was runner-up to Buffalo's great Gilles Perrault for the Calder Cup.

Hockey people do not envision an expansion team laying claim to the Stanley Cup for several more years. But if superstars are the key, perhaps the time is not too distant. There are some young men coming along — most of them just infants when Howe began his assault on the NHL record book — who are but a stride away from the elusive thing called stardom. Some of them are on expansion club rosters. Some are on the roster of the Minnesota North Stars.

At the conclusion of the Cup playoffs in 1971, Wren Blair once again assessed the accomplishments and potential of the stormy right winger he had taken from Boston four years earlier, and whom he had not given up on in the face of bitter criticism:

"I think Goldy is a semi-superstar now, based on his last two years. I still think he could be as good as Hull if everything fell for him. But I'm not for a minute saying that Goldy is out of the woods yet. He was greatly relieved that things ended as they did in 1971. But I have no guarantee that Goldy isn't going to spin off.

"On the other hand, if he continues to grow and mature, which he's done a lot of, he could go the other way, too, and become a really great hockey player."

Goldy, Danny Grant, the impressive young Drouin — all of these were considered superstar material coming off that big 1971 season. But still, Blair was not optimistic about achieving parity with some established clubs in the immediate future.

"I always said it would take a minimum of five years, and probably more like eight. When we lost to Montreal in the playoffs, we were still three to four years away from parity with teams like the Canadiens, Boston and New York — those three in particular."

Even so, there is this thirst every NHL team, expansion or not, has when training camp opens in the fall, and only a drink from that silver punch bowl will quench it.

When the season opens, there is a singular purpose that drives a team: to make the playoffs.

"If you don't make the playoffs, you don't get that chance for the Cup," said Goldy. "And you can't say in September that just because you made the second round of the playoffs the previous year that this year you will make it to the finals. Every year we made the playoffs we went right down to the last two or three weeks, battling for a spot. It's going to be tough every year because we have seven good clubs in the West, and it's just a matter of what kind of a start you get off to."

If the North Stars took anything important away from that 1971 season it was confidence. They had skated with the Stanley Cup champions and had played them on such terms that the outcome of the series had actually been in doubt. And that was something no expansion team had done before.

With that new confidence, the North Stars had most of the ingredients of which Stanley Cup winners are made: pride, determination, talent, unity of purpose. That they, as their expansion cousins, were short of experience, could only be left to the slow but steady progress of Father Time, or, as the case has been in so many instances, the rapid-fire trades of The Bird.

The Bird has a thirst for the Cup, too. Perhaps in the recesses of his mind, when he first began the painful process of building a National Hockey League team that might someday issue a sincere challenge for that big silver cup, he saw in that tempestuous blonde kid from Kitchener the spirit of which champions are made, and this was why he stubbornly refused to give up on Goldy.

The value of one man can, of course, be vastly overstated. The Chicago Black Hawks have not won the Stanley Cup since 1961, even with the mighty Hull.

Esposito, with his incredible 76 goals and backed by the one-time child wonder, Orr, were not enough to retain the Cup in 1971.

The North Stars may, in some near or distant time, drink deeply from Lord Stanley's silver mug, and it would be because they had assembled either the best or the most determined collection of hockey players in the NHL.

And perhaps on that unknown day, the winning goal will be delivered by a tall, intense gentleman with powerful shoulders, who dances into a happy shuffle as the puck ripples the net.

Then again, maybe Goldy will be watching that historic happening from the penalty box.

A Word From The Bird

An Epilogue

(Authors' Note: We have invited Wren Blair, general manager of the North Stars since their inception as an expansion team in the National Hockey League, to present his personal viewpoints on the brief history of the Minnesota organization. Since this book, in part, involves the development of a new major league hockey team from scratch, we felt the problems faced by a general manager of an expansion club, in so many ways, are much different from his counterparts on established NHL teams. Primarily, we asked him to comment on trials and tribulations in the formative years, the North Stars' progress to date, their dreams and goals and, of course, a word or two about Bill Goldsworthy.)

For those of us in management, building the North Stars from their very first breath in 1966 has been an exciting, albeit sometimes hectic, experience. Personally, I have found the assignment more exhausting and more difficult than I perhaps had anticipated. Still, that has made the challenge even more challenging, the excitement more exciting and, yes, has provided even more reason to rise up and fight back from discouragement and heartache.

One cannot feel that the original expansion draft of 1967 was, by any stretch of the imagination, liberal. The six old NHL clubs retained their first eleven players after which we were allowed to take one each. Then they froze a player, for a total of 12, and we had one, and so it continued.

Yet, that is the system in which we had to try to compete in those early years of expansion. A general manager attempting to build his team had to use every weapon at his disposal, including multiple trades, trading of draft choices and buying untried players (who were owned by NHL clubs and were on the Canadian or American Olympic teams) to slowly improve his roster.

In this regard I made many trades — probably more than any other expansion general manager. On some I was criticized. Still, I felt I was right, and in so believing made many moves forthwith. Obviously, I wasn't always right, but I felt that if I was right more often than I was wrong, the team had to get better, as I'm sure it has. The only person who doesn't incur criticism is the one who does nothing, and we had to do plenty!

Our talent in the early years, when I coached as well as managed, was such that only by pushing everyone to play over their heads could we hope to compete. Push them we did, and we did compete, because what we lacked in talent we made up for with sheer desire.

In that first year we played four games against each of the six original NHL clubs. Amazingly, we split with Boston and Detroit and went 1-1-2 with Chicago, Toronto and Montreal. Only New York

eluded us completely. Unbelievable, yet we did it.
How? By driving our players unmercifully, and, in
the process, driving ourselves unmercifully. The
NHL was new in Minnesota, and we felt this had to
be done to sell hockey here completely. Today the
popularity of the sport is very evident, and if I had it
to do over again, I would drive our initial club just as
hard if today's results could be the reward!

To this end a tremendous amount of credit must
go to the owners of the North Stars. They put in
untold hours preparing this community for the
advent to NHL hockey. Through thick and thin they
encouraged me and gave me my head to build a
team, especially in those early, trying days. Special
acclaim should be given to our president, Mr. Walter
Bush, Jr., and our team governor, Mr. Gordon Ritz,
with whom I worked closest. I wish to express my
sincere thanks to them for their confidence in me.
When we made trades that were criticized or second-
guessed, Walter and Gordy, along with Mr. Bob
McNulty, encouraged me to do what I felt was right,
regardless of outside influence. That type of confidence helps one stride forward at times when he
might otherwise doubt himself, and I am extremely
grateful for their encouragement.

Another gentleman I would like to single out for
special mention is my assistant, John Mariucci. We
hired John shortly after the formation of the North
Stars, and he has been a very loyal and close person,
particularly through those early, difficult days. He
typified "Mr. Hockey" in Minnesota at the beginning
of the North Stars and made my acclimation to the
community much easier. He appears to know

everyone in the state and introduced me to countless people who displayed much interest in the coming of the National Hockey League franchise. To this day, he is still a valued colleague in all of these areas, but even more important, I look on John as a close and valued friend.

I have spoken of excitement. Ah! What great nights they were — when we won our first game ever, against Los Angeles. What excitement the first time we defeated an old division club! How can you describe the excitement when we clinched a playoff spot that first year, and then when we won the first playoff round in the seventh and final game in Los Angeles to put us in the West Division finals against St. Louis. It was exciting to see Wayne Connelly score 35 goals that year, and to watch a youngster named Bill Goldsworthy battle his way through his first full NHL season and to know in your heart that, despite his turbulent nature, you were helping develop a future star. Yes, that is exciting, very exciting, and I was there, and especially proud to be there!

I spoke of discouragement — discouragement that first year when we lost that heart-breaking series in the seventh and final game in St. Louis after two periods of sudden death overtime; discouragement when I had the unhappy task of removing John Muckler as coach of the North Stars half-way through that bleak second season when, for some unknown reason, the team stumbled through 14 straight games without a win. Utter discouragement when we tumbled out of the playoffs that season. Discouraged and worried when the next season, shortly after Charlie Burns took over, the team went through a tortuous 20 games without a win. Yet, amazingly, after we suggested that Charlie return to the ice as a playing coach, the players grasped the ring he tossed them by his aggressive leadership on the ice and fought their way out of oblivion into a playoff spot.

I spoke of heartbreak. Yes, we've had more than our share of heartbreak on the North Stars, probably more than any other club in history in such a short span.

The tragic death of Bill Masterton touched us all deeply in that first year, so deeply in fact that those of us who were on that club are reluctant to discuss it even yet. However, let me say this: It was real heartbreak, and leading 20 young men back from that bitter experience, convincing them that life must go on, that the North Stars had a destiny, a cause and a goal was a challenge that I certainly had not counted on that first season. These were young people, most of whom had never faced a tragedy in their lives. Most of them were young enough that they had never lost a loved one, not their mother, father, sister or brother. No one that close. Yet suddenly, someone almost as close as you can get — a fellow teammate — was gone. Still the North Stars rallied and fought back with much of the leadership supplied by Carol Masterton, Bill's courageous young wife. To this day, Bill's memory is very special to the North Stars and Carol is one of our special favorites.

But heartbreak and tragedy hadn't left the North Stars. A 6:30 a.m. phone call late in 1970 from a shaken Tommy Williams once again deeply affected the lives of all of us on the club. The tragic death of Tommy's young and pretty wife, Emmy, had a solemn and sobering effect on all members of the team and their families. The painful loss so affected Tommy himself that calculated thinking by the executive members of the organization led all of us to the conclusion that only a new team, a new city and a completely new environment could help Tommy rehabilitate his fine hockey career. As before though, the team rallied under the solid leadership of Coach Jack Gordon. It went on to make the playoffs and finish with a tremendous showing when the North Stars became the first expansion team to ever beat an original NHL club in Stanley Cup competition. Additionally, we took the mighty Montreal Canadiens to six games before being eliminated.

As to our dreams and goals, I sincerely feel that our future looks bright. Exciting young hockey talent such as Fred Barrett, Gilles Gilbert, Barry Gibbs, Tom Reid, Dennis O'Brien, Buster Harvey, Jude Drouin, Terry Caffery, Ron Wilson, Gary Gambucci and Rod Norrish — all 24 years of age or younger — augers well for great hockey by the North Stars in the years that lie ahead.

Bill Goldsworthy and Danny Grant, both just in their mid-20's, stand on the threshold of superstardom if they work hard. Both have great shots, are fine skaters and can score goals with the best wingers in the NHL. Surround all of this by solid veteran performers such as Cesare Maniago, Ted Harris, Gump Worsley, Ted Hampson, J. P. Parise, Dennis Hextall, Bob Nevin, Lou Nanne, Charlie Burns and Doug Mohns, and one gets the feeling that this club has some fine talent — a blend, if you will, of youth, potential superstars and veteran performers.

The acquisition of Jack Gordon as coach moves us closer to achieving our goal. I spent considerable time trying to get Jack and was thoroughly delighted when those efforts were rewarded with his joining our organization last year. At that time I said "Jack will provide additional maturity to this team." I still feel the same way.

Let me, however, add a word of caution. As a result of our showing last season, many people are predicting even bigger things for the North Stars. I'm not quite clear about what they mean by bigger things, but I guess there are a couple: to be in the Stanley Cup Finals or to indeed win the Stanley Cup. I feel I am a strong competitor and my only goal in any league is to eventually win the ultimate. In the NHL that is the Stanley Cup. Realistically however, when one remembers that a mighty team like the New York Rangers has not won the Cup since 1939-40, more than 30 years ago, it reminds one of the sobering fact that we still are an expansion team, although I am sure we are a much better club than in the early days.

I said from the beginning that I felt it would take a minimum of seven years for us to reach parity with the established teams. This approximately parallels what happened to the Vikings in the NFL, and I still feel we have much work ahead. We are dedicated to taking this team even farther along the trail of development to a totally competitive NHL franchise. With such capable members of our scouting staff as Harold Cotton, Ted O'Connor, Gerald Blair, Leo

Boivin, John Mariucci, Bob Dill and Murray Williamson to assist our owners, Jack Gordon and myself, plus our network of area scouts, the hard work of minor league coaches John Muckler and Parker MacDonald, as well as all members of our front office staff and our trainers, Stan Waylett and "Doc" Rose, this organization is truly on the move.

As general manager of the North Stars, I am especially proud of the fact we are, to my knowledge, the only organization of the original six expansion clubs which has not replaced a single hockey executive since we started. We never have fired a member of our executive staff nor had a member of our staff quit our organization. I like to think this speaks strongly of the teamwork that exists at the executive level. It is my firm opinion that, to have a good team on the ice, the management, coaching and scouting staffs must also be a team off the ice. I further believe that the team is above all of us. The meaning of the word team goes beyond ownership, management, coaching or whatever because, to have a total team effort, the good of the team must come first and foremost no matter what tough decisions must be made.

Yes, the future does look bright. We will have our tough days and perhaps some disappointing seasons, but we are dedicated to making the best decisions we can. We are entitled, I suppose, to make limited mistakes as long as we can justify them with the philosophy that we felt we were doing the right thing for the team. More important to this community is the fact that we are trying to do the right things for the fans, because their tremendous interest in the

North Stars leads us to believe we have the finest
supporters in the country. Toward that goal we
dedicate our efforts.

And About Goldy

I have known Bill Goldsworthy for some time.
During the years I was with the Boston Bruins, he
was an aspiring youngster playing through our Junior
ranks. He was an outstanding player and I claimed
him in the expansion draft largely off my memories
of his exploits as a Junior A star with the Niagara
Falls Flyers. My logic was that players who are the
best in Junior A usually go on to be fine major
leaguers. Goldy had been a pro only a year or so
when the expansion draft took place and therefore
had had little chance to prove himself as a
professional.

I recall talking with Harry Sinden, a former
player of mine and long-time friend, immediately
following the expansion draft. Harry was then coach
of the Boston Bruins, the organization from which we
had claimed Goldy. "You took a great prospect in
Goldsworthy today," said Harry. "The only thing is
Goldy won't produce if you don't watch him. You
have to make him work, and if he does I think he can
be great."

I made up my mind that I would make him work
because, after all, hockey is a game of hard work,
and this becomes even more important when you
have ability such as Goldy has.

Of course, one has to remember that Bill was very
young at that time, and he was finding the struggle in
the National League much tougher with an expansion

club. I say that because, obviously, in the early years, an expansion club gets beaten in a lot of games and it can get you down — especially if you are a competitor as Goldy is. It hurts to lose and it affects you emotionally if it happens too often. Because I also hate to lose, sometimes our competitive natures clashed and the sparks flew between us.

As I look back, I think I had intense dreams on how great Goldy could be if he settled down and matured a bit. I think, in reality, I probably expected too much of him too fast. I am extremely fond of him as a person and I suspect, as with your own children, you demand more of those you care about.

Admittedly, I am a tough disciplinarian, but I make no apology for this. It is my firm opinion that discipline is a part of love, and if you care about your children, or others you must set an example for, you discipline them out of love in the hope that they will grow up to be able to face life's many battles. It would be easier to let things slide and shrug them off if you didn't care. I feel much the same way about hockey and the players who played for me. I have a great deal of respect and affection for all my players as well as those who ever have played for me. As a result, I have often found it very difficult to make trades. With every player you trade a little bit of yourself, emotionally, goes with him. To some that may be hard to believe, yet it is true. Still, the job must be done, and these emotions do not make it any easier.

In Goldy's case, our turbulent association at times, may have been because Bill had lost his father when he was quite young. I sometimes felt, as a result of this, that he might unconsciously resent male discipline. However, Goldy was always a fine youngster. A few times he would blow up, but this was usually during a game when he was under pressure.

Bill also is an instructor at our Haliburton Hockey Haven Boys Camp, and I am greatly impressed with his rapport with youngsters. They love him. The kids follow him around as though he is the Pied Piper. When children openly demonstrate affection for someone in this manner, you know he is a good person. And Goldy is.

Gradually he has improved his hockey with each season. Part of this improvement is because he is maturing more all the time. The past two seasons he has scored 71 goals for the North Stars, one of the best contributions made by a right winger in the NHL.

To continue on his way to stardom, Goldy must improve his defensive work and put more good games together consistently. He is unquestionably on the threshold of becoming a superstar if he continues on his present path. He is big and strong, skates powerfully and can shoot a puck better than most players in the game.

It has been a wonderful and gratifying experience to watch this young man grow and develop into a fine National League player. Even more important has been watching him grow as a man.

The North Stars also are growing into adulthood. We have many fine hockey players surrounding Goldy, who is one of only two originals left from that first expansion draft. The other is Goaltender Cesare Maniago.

As the club strives to progress from here, I'm sure we all hope that many more cheers emanate from the crowd as a big, blond right winger swoops in on goal, firing the puck into the net and then brings the crowd to its feet with another "Goldy Shuffle."

— Wren Blair
October, 1971

THEY WORE THE NORTH STAR

(GP — Games Played; G — Goals; A — Assists; TP — Total Points; PIM — Penalties in Minutes)

DAVE BALON (Forward)

| Season | | Regular Schedule | | | | | | Playoffs | | | |
	GP	G	A	TP	PIM	GP	G	A	TP	PIM
1967-68	73	15	32	47	84	14	4	9	13	14

Born Wakaw, Sask., August 2, 1938

FRED BARRETT (Defense)

| Season | | Regular Schedule | | | | | | Playoffs | | | |
	GP	G	A	TP	PIM	GP	G	A	TP	PIM
1970-71	57	0	13	13	75	—	—	—	—	—

Born Ottawa, Ont., January 26, 1950

BOB BARLOW (Forward)

| Season | | Regular Schedule | | | | | | Playoffs | | | |
	GP	G	A	TP	PIM	GP	G	A	TP	PIM
1969-70	70	16	17	33	10	6	2	2	4	6
1970-71	7	0	0	0	0	—	—	—	—	—

Born Hamilton, Ont., June 17, 1935

NORM BEAUDIN (Forward)

| Season | | Regular Schedule | | | | | | Playoffs | | | |
	GP	G	A	TP	PIM	GP	G	A	TP	PIM
1970-71	12	0	1	1	0	—	—	—	—	—

Born Montmartre, Sask., November 28, 1941

LEO BOIVIN (Defense)

Season	Regular Schedule					Playoffs				
	GP	G	A	TP	PIM	GP	G	A	TP	PIM
1968-69	28	1	6	7	16	–	–	–	–	–
1969-70	69	3	13	16	30	3	0	0	0	0

Born Prescott, Ont., August 2, 1932

ANDRE BOUDRIAS (Forward)

Season	Regular Schedule					Playoffs				
	GP	G	A	TP	PIM	GP	G	A	TP	PIM
1967-68	74	18	35	53	42	14	3	6	9	8
1968-69	53	4	9	13	6	–	–	–	–	–

Born Montreal, Que., September 19, 1943

CHARLIE BURNS (Forward)

Season	Regular Schedule					Playoffs				
	GP	G	A	TP	PIM	GP	G	A	TP	PIM
1969-70	50	3	13	16	10	6	1	0	1	0
1970-71	76	9	19	28	13	12	3	3	6	2

Born Detroit, Mich., February 14, 1936

TERRY CAFFERY (Forward)

Season	Regular Schedule					Playoffs				
	GP	G	A	TP	PIM	GP	G	A	TP	PIM
1970-71	8	0	0	0	0	1	0	0	0	0

Born Toronto, Ont., April 1, 1949

BOB CHARLEBOIS (Forward)

Season	Regular Schedule					Playoffs				
	GP	G	A	TP	PIM	GP	G	A	TP	PIM
1967-68	7	1	0	1	0	–	–	–	–	–

Born Cornwall, Ont., May 27, 1944

MIKE CHERNOFF (Forward)

Born Yorkton, Sask., May 13, 1946

Season	Regular Schedule					Playoffs				
	GP	G	A	TP	PIM	GP	G	A	TP	PIM
1968-69	1	0	0	0	0	–	–	–	–	–

BILL COLLINS (Forward)

Born Ottawa, Ont., July 13, 1943

Season	Regular Schedule					Playoffs				
	GP	G	A	TP	PIM	GP	G	A	TP	PIM
1967-68	71	9	11	20	41	10	2	4	6	4
1968-69	75	9	10	19	24	–	–	–	–	–
1969-70	74	29	9	38	48	6	0	1	1	8

WAYNE CONNELLY (Forward)

Born Rouyn, Que., December 16, 1939

Season	Regular Schedule					Playoffs				
	GP	G	A	TP	PIM	GP	G	A	TP	PIM
1967-68	74	35	21	56	40	14	8	3	11	2
1968-69	55	14	16	30	11	–	–	–	–	–

RAY CULLEN (Forward)

Born Ottawa, Ont., September 20, 1941

Season	Regular Schedule					Playoffs				
	GP	G	A	TP	PIM	GP	G	A	TP	PIM
1967-68	67	28	25	53	18	14	2	6	8	2
1968-69	67	26	38	64	44	6	1	4	5	0
1969-70	74	17	28	45	8					

GARY DINEEN (Forward)

Born Montreal, Que., December 24, 1943

Season	Regular Schedule					Playoffs				
	GP	G	A	TP	PIM	GP	G	A	TP	PIM
1968-69	4	0	1	1	0	–	–	–	–	–

JUDE DROUIN (Forward)

Born Mont-Louis, Que., October 28, 1948

Season	Regular Schedule						Playoffs			
	GP	G	A	TP	PIM	GP	G	A	TP	PIM
1970-71	75	16	52	68	49	12	5	7	12	10

GRANT ERICKSON (Forward)

Born Pierceland, Sask., April 28, 1947

Season	Regular Schedule						Playoffs			
	GP	G	A	TP	PIM	GP	G	A	TP	PIM
1969-70	4	0	0	0	0	—	—	—	—	—

SANDY FITZPATRICK (Forward)

Born Paisley, Scotland, December 22, 1944

Season	Regular Schedule						Playoffs			
	GP	G	A	TP	PIM	GP	G	A	TP	PIM
1967-68	18	3	6	9	6	12	0	0	0	0

GARY GELDART (Defense)

Born Moncton, N.B., June 14, 1951

Season	Regular Schedule						Playoffs			
	GP	G	A	TP	PIM	GP	G	A	TP	PIM
1970-71	4	0	0	0	5	—	—	—	—	—

BARRY GIBBS (Defense)

Born Lloydminster, Sask., September 28, 1948

Season	Regular Schedule						Playoffs			
	GP	G	A	TP	PIM	GP	G	A	TP	PIM
1969-70	56	3	13	16	182	6	1	0	1	7
1970-71	68	5	15	20	132	12	0	1	1	47

PETE GOEGAN (Defense)

Season	Regular Schedule					Playoffs				
	GP	G	A	TP	PIM	GP	G	A	TP	PIM
1967-68	46	1	2	3	30	—	—	—	—	—

Born Fort William, Ont., March 6, 1934

BILL GOLDSWORTHY (Forward)

Season	Regular Schedule					Playoffs				
	GP	G	A	TP	PIM	GP	G	A	TP	PIM
1967-68	68	14	19	33	68	14	8	7	15	12
1968-69	68	14	10	24	110	—	—	—	—	—
1969-70	75	36	29	65	89	6	4	3	7	6
1970-71	77	34	31	65	85	7	2	4	6	6

Born Kitchener, Ont., August 24, 1944

DANNY GRANT (Forward)

Season	Regular Schedule					Playoffs				
	GP	G	A	TP	PIM	GP	G	A	TP	PIM
1968-69	75	34	31	65	46	—	—	—	—	—
1969-70	76	29	28	57	23	6	0	2	2	4
1970-71	78	34	23	57	46	12	5	5	10	8

Born Fredericton, N.B., February 21, 1946

MURRAY HALL (Forward)

Season	Regular Schedule					Playoffs				
	GP	G	A	TP	PIM	GP	G	A	TP	PIM
1967-68	17	2	1	3	10	—	—	—	—	—

Born Kirkland Lake, Ont., November 24, 1940

TED HAMPSON (Forward)

Season	Regular Schedule					Playoffs				
	GP	G	A	TP	PIM	GP	G	A	TP	PIM
1970-71	18	4	6	10	4	11	3	3	6	0

Born Togo, Sask., December 11, 1936

DUKE HARRIS (Forward)

Born Sarnia, Ont., February 25, 1942

| | Regular Schedule | | | | | Playoffs | | | |
Season	GP	G	A	TP	PIM	GP	G	A	TP	PIM
1967-68	22	1	4	5	4	—	—	—	—	—

TED HARRIS (Defense)

Born Winnipeg, Man., July 18, 1936

| | Regular Schedule | | | | | Playoffs | | | |
Season	GP	G	A	TP	PIM	GP	G	A	TP	PIM
1970-71	78	2	13	15	130	12	0	4	4	36

BUSTER HARVEY (Forward)

Born Fredericton, N.B., April 2, 1950

| | Regular Schedule | | | | | Playoffs | | | |
Season	GP	G	A	TP	PIM	GP	G	A	TP	PIM
1970-71	59	12	8	20	36	7	0	0	0	4

BILL HEINDL (Forward)

Born Sherbrooke, Quebec, May 13, 1946

| | Regular Schedule | | | | | Playoffs | | | |
Season	GP	G	A	TP	PIM	GP	G	A	TP	PIM
1970-71	12	1	1	2	0	—	—	—	—	—

LARRY HILLMAN (Defense)

Born Kirkland Lake, Ont., February 5, 1937

| | Regular Schedule | | | | | Playoffs | | | |
Season	GP	G	A	TP	PIM	GP	G	A	TP	PIM
1968-69	12	1	5	6	0	—	—	—	—	—

WAYNE HILLMAN (Defense)

Born Kirkland Lake, Ont., November 13, 1938

| | Regular Schedule | | | | | Playoffs | | | |
Season	GP	G	A	TP	PIM	GP	G	A	TP	PIM
1968-69	50	0	8	8	32	—	—	—	—	—

BRONCO HORVATH (Forward)

Season	Regular Schedule					Playoffs				
	GP	G	A	TP	PIM	GP	G	A	TP	PIM
1967-68	14	1	6	7	4	—	—	—	—	—

Born Port Colborne, Ont., March 12, 1930

DON JOHNS (Defense)

Season	Regular Schedule					Playoffs				
	GP	G	A	TP	PIM	GP	G	A	TP	PIM
1967-68	4	0	0	0	6	—	—	—	—	—

Born St. George, Ont., December 13, 1937

JOEY JOHNSTON (Forward)

Season	Regular Schedule					Playoffs				
	GP	G	A	TP	PIM	GP	G	A	TP	PIM
1968-69	12	1	0	1	6	—	—	—	—	—

Born Peterborough, Ont., March 3, 1949

MARSHALL JOHNSTON (Forward)

Season	Regular Schedule					Playoffs				
	GP	G	A	TP	PIM	GP	G	A	TP	PIM
1967-68	7	0	0	0	0	—	—	—	—	—
1968-69	13	0	0	0	2	—	—	—	—	—
1969-70	28	0	5	5	14	6	0	0	0	2
1970-71	1	0	0	0	0	—	—	—	—	—

Born Birch Hills, Sask., June 6, 1941

GORDON LABOSSIERE

Season	Regular Schedule					Playoffs				
	GP	G	A	TP	PIM	GP	G	A	TP	PIM
1970-71	29	8	4	12	4	3	0	0	0	4

Born St. Boniface, Man., January 2, 1940

CLAUDE LAROSE (Forward)

Season	Regular Schedule					Playoffs				
	GP	G	A	TP	PIM	GP	G	A	TP	PIM
1968-69	67	25	37	62	106	—	—	—	—	—
1969-70	75	24	23	47	109	6	1	1	2	25

Born Hearst, Ont., March 2, 1942

DANNY LAWSON (Forward)

Season	Regular Schedule					Playoffs				
	GP	G	A	TP	PIM	GP	G	A	TP	PIM
1968-69	18	3	3	6	4	—	—	—	—	—
1969-70	45	9	8	17	19	6	0	1	1	2
1970-71	33	1	5	6	2	10	0	0	0	0

Born Toronto, Ont., October 30, 1947

LEN LUNDE (Forward)

Season	Regular Schedule					Playoffs				
	GP	G	A	TP	PIM	GP	G	A	TP	PIM
1967-68	7	0	1	1	0	—	—	—	—	—

Born Campbell River, B.C., November 13, 1936

PARKER MACDONALD (Forward)

Season	Regular Schedule					Playoffs				
	GP	G	A	TP	PIM	GP	G	A	TP	PIM
1967-68	69	19	23	42	22	14	4	5	9	2
1968-69	35	2	9	11	0	—	—	—	—	—

Born Sydney, N.S., June 14, 1933

BARRIE MACKENZIE (Defense)

Season	Regular Schedule					Playoffs				
	GP	G	A	TP	PIM	GP	G	A	TP	PIM
1968-69	6	0	1	1	6	—	—	—	—	—

Born Toronto, Ont., August 16, 1941

MILAN MARCETTA (Forward)

Season	Regular Schedule					Playoffs				
	GP	G	A	TP	PIM	GP	G	A	TP	PIM
1967-68	36	4	13	17	6	14	7	7	14	4
1968-69	18	3	2	5	4	—	—	—	—	—

Born Cadomin, Alta., September 19, 1936

BILL MASTERTON (Forward)

Season	Regular Schedule					Playoffs				
	GP	G	A	TP	PIM	GP	G	A	TP	PIM
1967-68	38	4	8	12	4	—	—	—	—	—

Born Winnipeg, Man., August 16, 1938

BRIAN McBRATNEY (Defense)

Season	Regular Schedule					Playoffs				
	GP	G	A	TP	PIM	GP	G	A	TP	PIM
1967-68	1	0	0	0	2	—	—	—	—	—
1968-69	5	0	1	1	2	—	—	—	—	—

Born Toronto, Ont., December 27, 1951

TED McCASKILL (Forward)

Season	Regular Schedule					Playoffs				
	GP	G	A	TP	PIM	GP	G	A	TP	PIM
1967-68	4	0	2	2	0	—	—	—	—	—

Born Kapusking, Ont., October 29, 1936

BOB McCORD (Defense)

Season	Regular Schedule					Playoffs				
	GP	G	A	TP	PIM	GP	G	A	TP	PIM
1967-68	70	3	9	12	39	14	2	5	7	10
1968-69	69	4	17	21	70	—	—	—	—	—

Born Matheson, Ont., March 30, 1934

WALT MCKECHNIE (Forward)

Season	Regular Schedule					Playoffs				
	GP	G	A	TP	PIM	GP	G	A	TP	PIM
1967-68	4	0	0	0	0	9	3	2	5	0
1968-69	58	5	9	14	22	—	—	—	—	—
1969-70	20	1	3	4	21	—	—	—	—	—
1970-71	30	3	1	4	34	—	—	—	—	—

Born London, Ont., June 19, 1947

MIKE MCMAHON (Defense)

Season	Regular Schedule					Playoffs				
	GP	G	A	TP	PIM	GP	G	A	TP	PIM
1967-68	74	14	33	47	71	14	3	7	10	4
1968-69	43	0	11	11	21	—	—	—	—	—

Born Quebec, Que., August 30, 1941

BARRIE MEISSNER (Forward)

Season	Regular Schedule					Playoffs				
	GP	G	A	TP	PIM	GP	G	A	TP	PIM
1967-68	1	0	0	0	2	—	—	—	—	—
1968-69	5	0	1	1	2	—	—	—	—	—

Born Unity, Sask., July 26, 1946

JOHN MISZUK (Defense)

Season	Regular Schedule					Playoffs				
	GP	G	A	TP	PIM	GP	G	A	TP	PIM
1969-70	50	0	6	6	51	—	—	—	—	—

Born Naliboki, Poland, Sept. 29, 1940

DOUG MOHNS (Defense-Forward)

Season	Regular Schedule					Playoffs				
	GP	G	A	TP	PIM	GP	G	A	TP	PIM
1970-71	17	2	5	7	14	6	2	2	4	10

Born Capreol, Ont., December 13, 1933

WAYNE MULOIN (Defense)

Season	Regular Schedule					Playoffs				
	GP	G	A	TP	PIM	GP	G	A	TP	PIM
1970-71	7	0	0	0	6	7	0	0	0	2

Born Dryden, Ont., December 24, 1941

LOU NANNE (Defense-Forward)

Season	Regular Schedule					Playoffs				
	GP	G	A	TP	PIM	GP	G	A	TP	PIM
1967-68	2	0	1	1	0	—	—	—	—	—
1968-69	41	2	12	14	47	—	—	—	—	—
1969-70	74	3	20	23	75	5	0	2	2	2
1970-71	68	5	11	16	22	12	3	6	9	4

Born Sault Ste. Marie, Ont., June 2, 1941

DENNIS O'BRIEN (Defense)

Season	Regular Schedule					Playoffs				
	GP	G	A	TP	PIM	GP	G	A	TP	PIM
1970-71	27	3	2	5	29	9	0	0	0	20

Born Port Hope, Ont., June 10, 1949

MURRAY OLIVER (Forward)

Season	Regular Schedule					Playoffs				
	GP	G	A	TP	PIM	GP	G	A	TP	PIM
1970-71	61	9	23	32	8	12	7	4	11	0

Born Hamilton, Ont., November 14, 1937

BILL ORBAN (Forward)

Season	Regular Schedule					Playoffs				
	GP	G	A	TP	PIM	GP	G	A	TP	PIM
1968-69	21	1	5	6	10	—	—	—	—	—
1969-70	9	0	2	2	7	—	—	—	—	—

Born Regina, Sask., February 20, 1944

DANNY O'SHEA (Forward)

Season	Regular Schedule						Playoffs			
	GP	G	A	TP	PIM	GP	G	A	TP	PIM
1968-69	74	15	34	49	88	–	–	–	–	–
1969-70	75	10	24	34	82	6	1	0	1	8
1970-71	59	14	12	26	16	–	–	–	–	–

Born Toronto, Ont., June 14, 1945

J. P. PARISE (Forward)

Season	Regular Schedule						Playoffs			
	GP	G	A	TP	PIM	GP	G	A	TP	PIM
1968-69	76	22	27	49	57	–	–	–	–	–
1969-70	74	24	48	72	72	6	3	2	5	2
1970-71	73	11	23	34	60	12	3	3	6	22

Born Smooth Rock Falls, Ont., December 11, 1941

BILL PLAGER (Defense)

Season	Regular Schedule						Playoffs			
	GP	G	A	TP	PIM	GP	G	A	TP	PIM
1967-68	32	0	2	2	30	12	0	2	2	8

Born Kirkland Lake, Ont., July 6, 1945

TOM POLANIC (Defense)

Season	Regular Schedule						Playoffs			
	GP	G	A	TP	PIM	GP	G	A	TP	PIM
1969-70	16	0	2	2	53	5	1	1	2	4
1970-71	3	0	0	0	0	–	–	–	–	–

Born Toronto, Ont., April 2, 1943

ANDRE PRONOVOST (Forward)

Season	Regular Schedule						Playoffs			
	GP	G	A	TP	PIM	GP	G	A	TP	PIM
1967-68	8	0	0	0	0	–	–	–	–	–

Born Shawinigan Falls, Que., July 22, 1935

DICK REDMOND (Defense)

Season	Regular Schedule					Playoffs				
	GP	G	A	TP	PIM	GP	G	A	TP	PIM
1969-70	7	0	1	1	4	—	—	—	—	—

Born Kirkland Lake, Ont., August 14, 1949

TOM REID (Defense)

Season	Regular Schedule					Playoffs				
	GP	G	A	TP	PIM	GP	G	A	TP	PIM
1968-69	18	0	4	4	38	—	—	—	—	—
1969-70	66	1	7	8	51	6	0	1	1	4
1970-71	73	3	14	17	62	12	0	6	6	20

Born Fort Erie, Ont., June 24, 1946

DUANE RUPP (Defense)

Season	Regular Schedule					Playoffs				
	GP	G	A	TP	PIM	GP	G	A	TP	PIM
1968-69	29	2	1	3	8	—	—	—	—	—

Born Macnutt, Sask., March 29, 1938

DARRYL SLY (Defense)

Season	Regular Schedule					Playoffs				
	GP	G	A	TP	PIM	GP	G	A	TP	PIM
1969-70	29	1	0	1	6	—	—	—	—	—

Born Collingwood, Ont., April 3, 1939

BRIAN SMITH (Forward)

Season	Regular Schedule					Playoffs				
	GP	G	A	TP	PIM	GP	G	A	TP	PIM
1968-69	9	0	1	1	0	—	—	—	—	—

Born Ottawa, Ont., September 6, 1940

GEORGE STANDING (Forward)

Season		Regular Schedule						Playoffs			
	GP	G	A	TP	PIM		GP	G	A	TP	PIM
1967-68	2	0	0	0	0		—	—	—	—	—

Born Toronto, Ont., August 3, 1941

JEAN-GUY TALBOT (Defense)

Season		Regular Schedule						Playoffs			
	GP	G	A	TP	PIM		GP	G	A	TP	PIM
1967-68	4	0	0	0	4		—	—	—	—	—

Born Cap de la Madeleine, Que., July 11, 1932

TED TAYLOR (Forward)

Season		Regular Schedule						Playoffs			
	GP	G	A	TP	PIM		GP	G	A	TP	PIM
1967-68	31	3	5	8	34		—	—	—	—	—

Born Brandon, Manitoba, February 25, 1942

LEO THIFFAULT (Forward)

Season		Regular Schedule						Playoffs			
	GP	G	A	TP	PIM		GP	G	A	TP	PIM
1967-68	—	—	—	—	—		5	0	0	0	0

Born Drummondville, Que., December 16, 1944

ELMER VASKO (Defense)

Season		Regular Schedule						Playoffs			
	GP	G	A	TP	PIM		GP	G	A	TP	PIM
1967-68	70	1	6	7	45		14	0	2	2	6
1968-69	72	1	7	8	68		—	—	—	—	—
1969-70	3	0	0	0	0		—	—	—	—	—

Born Duparquet, Ont., December 11, 1935

BOB WHITLOCK (Forward)

Season	Regular Schedule					Playoffs				
	GP	G	A	TP	PIM	GP	G	A	TP	PIM
1969-70	1	0	0	0	0	—	—	—	—	—

Born Charlottetown, P.E.I., July 16, 1949

TOM WILLIAMS (Forward)

Season	Regular Schedule					Playoffs				
	GP	G	A	TP	PIM	GP	G	A	TP	PIM
1969-70	75	15	52	67	18	6	1	5	6	0
1970-71	41	10	18	28	37	—	—	—	—	—

Born Duluth, Minn., April 17, 1940

BOB WOYTOWICH (Defense)

Season	Regular Schedule					Playoffs				
	GP	G	A	TP	PIM	GP	G	A	TP	PIM
1967-68	66	4	17	21	63	14	0	1	1	18

Born Winnipeg, Man., August 18, 1941

GOALTENDER RECORDS

(GP — Games Played; GA — Goals Against; SO — Shutouts; AVE. — Average)

GARY BAUMAN

Season	Regular Schedule				Playoffs			
	GP	GA	SO	AVE.	GP	GA	SO	AVE.
1967-68	22	75	0	3.41	—	—	—	—
1968-69	5	22	0	4.40	—	—	—	—

Born Innisfail, Alta., July 21, 1940

KEN BRODERICK

Season	Regular Schedule				Playoffs			
	GP	GA	SO	AVE.	GP	GA	SO	AVE.
1969-70	4½	26	0	6.00	—	—	—	—

Born Toronto, Ont., February 16, 1942

GILLES GILBERT

Season	Regular Schedule				Playoffs			
	GP	GA	SO	AVE.	GP	GA	SO	AVE.
1969-70	1	6	0	6.00	—	—	—	—
1970-71	17	59	0	3.80	—	—	—	—

Born St. Esprit, Que., March 31, 1949

CESARE MANIAGO

Season	Regular Schedule				Playoffs			
	GP	GA	SO	AVE.	GP	GA	SO	AVE.
1967-68	48	133	6	2.77	14-2/3	39	0	2.62
1968-69	60	198	1	3.30	—	—	—	—
1969-70	48-1/6	163	2	3.38	3	6	1	2.00
1970-71	40	107	5	2.69	8	28	0	3.50

Born Trail, B.C., January 13, 1939

FERN RIVARD

Season	Regular Schedule				Playoffs			
	GP	GA	SO	AVE.	GP	GA	SO	AVE.
1968-69	11	48	0	4.38	—	—	—	—
1969-70	13-1/3	42	1	3.15	—	—	—	—

Born Grand' Mere, Que., January 18, 1946

CARL WETZEL

Season	Regular Schedule				Playoffs			
	GP	GA	SO	AVE.	GP	GA	SO	AVE.
1967-68	4½	18	0	4.00	—	—	—	—

Born Detroit, Mich., December 12, 1938

LORNE (GUMP) WORSLEY

Season	Regular Schedule				Playoffs			
	GP	GA	SO	AVE.	GP	GA	SO	AVE.
1969-70	7½	20	1	2.65	3	14	0	4.67
1970-71	24	57	0	2.49	3	13	0	3.25

Born Montreal, Que., May 14, 1929